W9-BON-565

The lovely Giulietta Sprint Zagato has it all—style, lightness, grace and a successful racing legacy. It is the essence of the exotic postwar Alfa. Author photo.

Joe Benson

Illustrated
ALFA ROMEO
BUYER'S
GUIDE

Motorbooks International
Publishers & Wholesalers Inc.
Osceola, Wisconsin 54020, USA ®

ACKNOWLEDGMENTS

I would like to acknowledge the contributions of all those who assisted and encouraged me in this effort with their photographs, time and knowledge. Particular thanks to:

Jeanette Benson, my wonderful and understanding wife; Russ Baer; Richard Baron of *Road & Track*; Pat Braden; Jean Brindamour; Don Bruno; Don Ereminas, of Ereminas Imports Inc.; Mike Hemsley; Don Hughes; Mike Ryan; Bob Schneider of *The Sports Car Exchange*; Bob Schnittger; Steve Schwartz; Scott Shadle; Tom Tann; Jim Weber of Alfa Romeo, Inc.; Henry Wessels III; *Alfa Romeo—All Cars From 1910*, by Luigi Fusi.

Joe Benson

First published in 1983 by Motorbooks International Publishers & Wholesalers Inc, PO Box 2, 729 Prospect Avenue, Osceola, WI 54020 USA

© Joe Benson, 1983

Motorbooks International is a certified trademark, registered with the United States Patent Office

Printed and bound in the United States of America

The information in this book is true and complete to the best of our knowledge. All recommendations are made without any guarantee on the part of the author or publisher, who also disclaim any liability incurred in connection with the use of this data or specific details

Library of Congress Cataloging in Publication Data

Benson, Joe
  Illustrated Alfa Romeo buyer's guide.

  1. Alfa Romeo automobile—Purchasing.   I. Title.
TL215.A35B46 1983   629.2'222   83-5326
ISBN 0-87938-163-9 (pbk.)

Front cover photo: Front-fender marker lights tell us that these are a pair of 101-Series Giulias. A Sprint (1962-64) on the left, a Sprint Speciale (1963-65) on the right at Monza in northern Italy. Tim Parker photo.

Motorbooks International books are also available at discounts in bulk quantity for industrial or sales-promotional use. For details write to Special Sales Manager at the Publisher's address

INTRODUCTION

"An Alfa Romeo? Who makes that?" is a response all too familiar to U.S. owners of this most interesting marque. A patient group, these owners frequently take the educational approach, explaining that Alfa Romeos are build by Alfa Romeo S.p.A., an Italian car manufacturer. It is one of the oldest companies in the business, with origins reaching back to the beginnings of the century.

The "Alfa" part of the name is an acronym for "Anonima Lombarda Fabbrica Automobili," a reflection of its beginnings as an Italian assembly group for the French Darracq automobile. The "Romeo" portion was added by Nicola Romeo, an Italian industrialist, when he took over the company in 1920. It was under his direction that Alfa seriously turned to competition to promote the sales of its cars and improve their durability.

It would be an understatement to merely say it was a successful venture. In the years between the two world wars, Alfa Romeo established itself as one of the truly great producers of exotic sport and racing machinery, and a listing of its designers and drivers reads like a Who's Who of motorsports. But these early handmade Alfas were built in relatively limited numbers, and were quite expensive and beyond the reach of all but the very wealthy.

In the process of rebuilding after World War II, Alfa Romeo pursued a trend it had begun earlier to smaller and more affordable cars. The success of the Giulietta series opened the doors to large-scale production, and the subsequent success and proliferation of models are the subject matter of this book.

Today Alfa Romeo's annual production figures exceed 100,000 vehicles, and the company is diversified into racing, research, aeronautical, commercial vehicle and automotive components divisions. It is also a holding of the Italian government, and has been since the end of World War I when Alfa was taken into the IRI, or Industrial Reconstruction Institute. Having grown into a major European producer, Alfa still remains relatively unknown to most Americans, a result of being imported in fairly small numbers of several thousand a year plus a very minimal advertising program.

But while Alfa Romeo's history is fascinating, it is the cars themselves we are primarily concerned with here. Whether your interest in them is casual or serious, I hope this guide provides an accurate and useful understanding of the postwar Alfas, their characteristics, quirks and personalities. But it's only fair to warn you in advance of their addictive nature. The American Alfa club unashamedly exploits this quality by gladly admitting nonowners, confident that once exposed, it's only a matter of time.

If there is one thing that characterizes Alfa Romeos, it is the excellence and continuity of design lavished on their engines. They are unmistakably the product of racers and engineers caught up in the artistic possibilities of internal combustion. Their throaty induction sounds and healthy exhaust burbles leave little doubt as to their free-breathing, spirited nature. While Henry Ford was building the Model T, Alfa Romeo was routinely turning out supercharged twin cam powerplants in exquisitely cast aluminum. In the present postwar period, this same philosophy is still evident, and is the Alfa's primary attraction to the enthusiast. Ask any owner about his car, and invariably the hood will be raised.

More subtle but equally important is Alfa's approach to chassis design. Without exception, the brakes are excellent and fully up to the demands of racing. On the street, they permit the driver to be a spectator rather than participant in most accident situations. While Alfas corner with lots of body lean, they do so with no loss of smoothness or precision. Biased toward understeer, they handle so predictably that novice and expert alike can routinely push them to their limits without embarrassment or fatigue. They're really great fun to drive, and their deliberately overdesigned mechanicals actually thrive on the hard usage they encourage.

Alfa Romeo may very well have been the first company to take a serious approach to the small performance car, giving it the quality and features normally reserved for more expensive sporting machinery. As a result, these cars have come to occupy a unique market niche as affordable and usable exotics, with specification sheets that read like an enthusiast's wish-list.

What kind of person buys an Alfa Romeo? Demographic studies indicate owners tend to be well educated and usually in a professional field, with a high percentage in technical pursuits. Yet some used models are so reasonably priced that it is not unusual to find students driving them as "starter" sports cars. In other words, if you really want an Alfa, there's something in almost every price range, from the mortgage-your-house rarity to the please-tow-it-away special.

Contrary to popular belief, you don't have to be a mechanic or engineer to successfully own an Alfa, although a sensitive ear does help. Many buy an Alfa never intending to do any of the maintenance, then find the straightforward elegance of the design luring them into more and more of the servicing. I've often suspected that a significant number of Alfa engines are needlessly rebuilt just because it's such an easy and rewarding task, and the tendency of owners to become perfectionists.

Alfas do have their problems, of course, all of which are manageable with a little knowledge and common sense. But then no car ever is perfect, so you choose them according to what they offer and what you're willing to put up with. Alfas cater to the enthusiast with a sense of mechanical esthetics and an appreciation of tradition. If you fit this description, you will probably find an Alfa to be a most satisfying adventure.

As this *Illustrated Alfa Romeo Buyer's Guide* goes to press, Alfa Romeo itself is for sale. Thirteen straight years of loss, plus a troublesome union, have forced a decision by the Italian government to return Alfa Romeo to the private sector as the quickest cure for its financial problems.

However, in all fairness, it was most likely the government's own directive to Alfa to industrialize southern Italy with the Alfasud project that contributed most heavily to the present plight. This becomes particularly apparent when considering that the Alfasud was introduced in 1973, exactly thirteen years ago. In addition, the government's strong reluctance over the years to deal firmly with Alfa's unions, for fear of generating a political crisis, fostered operational problems.

A number of other auto companies including GM, Chrysler and Fiat considered and then declined the opportunity to acquire Alfa. More recently, Ford has been the principal contender, although Fiat has indicated it is preparing a counter-proposal. If accepted, Ford's announced intent is to upgrade and continue all of Alfa's plants and eventually bring them to full capacity of around 400,000 vehicles annually.

There is both opportunity and peril for Alfa in such arrangements. With a Ford takeover, the best outcome would see Ford maintain and enhance Alfa's prestigious name and possibly return it to the very expensive exoticar market. Ford would also use Alfa as its performance-car-development center. Ford's strong worldwide sales network could also be opened to Alfa, solving the distribution problem facing any low-volume producer. The worst outcome would see Alfa eventually reduced to a specialty nameplate on a Ford product.

An example of both approaches can be seen in the manner that Fiat has already handled its acquisitions of Lancia and Ferrari. Lancia has been reduced to, outwardly, a special-bodied Fiat while Ferrari production has thrived and maintained its unique identity and componentry.

Of course, if all talks fail to produce a buyer, Alfa may be left to solve its own difficulties. One possible solution would be to sell the difficult divisions, such as the Alfasud plant, and concentrate on the profitable models. Nissan could be a prospective buyer because of its involvement with the ARNA vehicle which used Alfasud running gear in a Nissan body. However, the government may not want to give a Japanese automaker such easy access to the presently restricted Italian market.

Whatever the outcome, Alfa has enriched and influenced the automotive scene well beyond what its mere production numbers would ever suggest. Economic brinkmanship has been a facet of Alfa's automotive existence from the very beginning when Nicola Romeo first rescued the company. Perhaps one of the secrets behind Alfa's remarkable ability over the years to design cars that lead trends rather than follow is that its survival has always desperately depended on it. As enthusiasts we should wish Alfa well, and hope the solution that is found allows its special creativity to remain available to us long into the future.

TABLE OF CONTENTS

FINDING, INSPECTING, RESTORING AND ENJOYING AN ALFA

Once you decide to buy an Alfa, the adventure begins. If one of the new models has caught your eye, well, that's easy. Your local, friendly dealer will be delighted to sell you one. But don't be surprised to find him quizzing you on your driving habits and automotive knowledge. Alfas, you see, are not for just anyone. Many a conscientious dealer has steered an inappropriate potential buyer into something more mundane, saving both of them a lot of unhappiness.

Dealers can also be quite helpful in finding a good used Alfa, but there are many other excellent sources as well. The local Alfa club members will usually have the better-maintained cars in an area, but they also tend to know the real values, and generally do not give them away. As usual, you get what you pay for. The classified ads of the national Alfa club are literally a gold mine of interesting cars and parts, but quite often require a bit of travel to retrieve your find.

Don't overlook the classified ads of the newspapers in your area. A wide selection of Alfas seem to turn up there, and frequently prove to be excellent bargains. All too often Alfas, as well as other sports cars, are purchased by people without the slightest hint of mechanical sensitivity, who soon reduce them to poorly maintained, nonstarting disappointments. If you are at all handy with Alfas, and they are quite easy to work on, this type of vehicle is unquestionably your best buy. Usually a few weeks of attention is all that's required to put one right again.

There are also the ads in the enthusiast publications, but these, too, are national in scope. It always seems the best-sounding vehicles are quite far away, but sometimes it can be worth the trip. The most useful magazines for Alfa-searching seem to be *Hemmings Motor News, Autoweek* and *Road & Track.*

If it's an older or specialty Alfa that you're after, all of the above sources still apply, but there may be a much better way: If the model you want happens to have its own registry, by all means join and correspond.

Then again, some people just seem to fall into Alfa ownership without even trying. I know of one fellow whose uncle left him a perfect-condition 6C-2500 Farina-bodied Super Sport Cabriolet. He doesn't know much about Alfas, but likes the unique character of the car, considers it a family keepsake and absolutely refuses to consider selling it. And apparently one of the 1900 BAT owners bought his winged wonder from a corner used-car lot. He then proceeded to drive it for several years as an everyday car, gradually coming to realize it was something very special.

If you should manage to find and buy the Alfa of your dreams, I wish you the same luck and enjoyment that I've had with mine. You may also find out what most owners eventually realize—that it soon becomes impossible to possess just one. I'm on my fifteenth Alfa now, four of which I still own. They're an absolute addiction, and if you haven't already been "hooked," it's only fair to warn you in advance.

The key to happiness when buying an older Alfa is to determine in advance exactly what you are getting. Even a car in truly wretched condition can be a pleasant purchase if it suits your needs and you pay a fair price.

But if your goal is to acquire an Alfa that is immediately usable with a minimum of extra expense, a few precautions are in order. If it is being sold by a dealer, sometimes he or she will provide a short-term warranty—usually ninety days—against major failures.

When buying from a private party, there are several possible ways to assure yourself of the car's condition. The best is to have the owner take it to a dealer or perhaps to your favorite repair shop. For the cost of an hour or two of shop time, you can have performed what is usually called a "prepurchase inspection." You end up with a professional's opinion of the car, some test data and, frequently, the chance to check out the underside of the car while it's up on a hoist. If problems are found, they can then be part of the price negotiation. Be extremely cautious if an owner won't agree to this type of arrangement—he usually has something to hide.

The next best approach is to bring along a friend who is reasonably familiar with the Alfa model in question, and can help you spot problem areas. The Alfa club provides many such contacts for this type of assistance, and is one of the many reasons for joining.

Occasionally time will simply not permit the luxury of outside help. The really good deals are usually scooped up so fast that hesitation means missing out. While this is just an irritation with a production vehicle, losing a really rare Alfa through indecision can be truly depressing. To be successful in such a venture, you have to first educate yourself in the pricing and quirks of the desired model, and then be prepared to pounce when your instincts say "Go!"

Fortunately, despite their exotic nature and components, Alfas are very simple and straight-forward mechanically. That's why so many owners do their own servicing. These same characteristics also make it not too difficult to verify a used Alfa's condition before you buy.

A test drive is always recommended if at all possible. Begin very slowly and gently, and let the subtle items reveal themselves—the steering play, brake pull, imbalances and unusual noise kind of items. Pick up the pace and see how the car reacts to being pushed hard—look for things like clutch slip, braking roughness, overheating, high-rpm miss, worn synchronizers and driveline noise. Check under the hood with the engine idling for oil or coolant leaks.

For corrosion, check around on the back side of the rocker panels (they're a double-walled chamber on an Alfa), the ends of the rockers in the wheelwells, the low points in the floorpan (the foot-wells and seatwells), the rear suspension-link attachment points, the inside bottoms of the doors and the rear inner wheelwells along the flange. On an Alfetta, check the sheetmetal in the engine compart-ment above and to the rear of the wheel arch. In a vehicle with a recessed spare-tire well, remove the spare to be sure that trapped water has not rusted the bottom pan.

All convertible-top cars should have particular attention paid to the entire floorpan structure. Note that an Alfa usually has very dense insulating mats under the carpet which makes it difficult to check for floor rot from inside the car. Once soaked, these mats will hold water for a long time; slip your hand under the carpet in low areas and check for moisture.

The most common Alfa mechanical problem is a failed head gasket. This is not difficult to fix, but the repair cost should be considered. In the early stages, oil will drool down the left rear side of the block immediately after a cold start. As it progresses, oil will eventually show up in the coolant; remove the radiator cap and check for oily scum. The later cars will also accumulate this goo in the coolant over-flow bottle.

Occasionally coolant will get into the oil. A froth resembling a chocolate milk shake on the inside of the oil fill-cap is the symptom. This could result from a gasket leak, but more typically it is from a failed seal between a cylinder liner and the block, a more expensive repair.

If the compression seal around a cylinder is failing, the cooling system will be over-pressurized and the coolant slowly blown out. Overflow bottles will tend to fill up and spill over. Eventually the head can overheat and warp if this condition goes unchecked. Remove the radiator cap and check for the smell of combustion products and watch for bubbling from the upper radiator hose area as con-firmation of this problem.

Yes, Alfas and other rare cars can still be found tucked away and seemingly forgotten in out-of-the-way barns. Author photo.

Even GTA Juniors can be crunched, but the car's uniqueness easily justifies the repair expense. If this had been a production steel-bodied GTV, such an accident would probably result in it being de-clared a "total." John Hoard photo.

On Spica injected cars, look for a reasonably quick cold start, and then smooth running under both cold and fully warm conditions. Check the throttle bellcrank on the intake manifold for smooth rotation and a full return to the idle stop without any traces of binding. Check the dipstick for the smell of gasoline—that would indicate failed seals around the pump plungers and would be very expensive to repair. When the ignition is turned on, the rear fuel pump should immediately be heard and the pressure warning light merely blink on and off to indicate normal operation.

If a Spica injected Alfa should refuse to start or runs poorly, don't panic. In most cases, simple linkage, sensor and richness adjustments—in other words a tune-up—are all that's required. For such situations, if you're not familiar with the injection system yourself, be sure to have it checked over by someone who is, to eliminate the possibility of a costly injection pump replacement.

In Alfa gearboxes, the second-gear synchronizer is usually the first to go. If it doesn't "grunch" too badly, several successive changes of transmission lubricant will work wonders. If all the synchronizers are bad in a pre-1969 Alfa, most likely an EP-additive gear lube was used which provided the wrong friction characteristics. For these cases, several flushes of the correct lubricant will usually restore normal operation.

During the road test, let off the throttle in each gear, including reverse, to make sure the shift lever does not hop out of engagement. While this can indicate a bent shift fork, it is also caused by misaligned shift boots.

In all cases, try to retain your objectivity and apply the same standards and inspection techniques as you would for any other car. Occasionally this can be very difficult when the seller's phone is ringing off the hook with inquiries, and other potential buyers are standing in the driveway. Always try to imagine how you will feel about this particular purchase a month or even a year later, and keep in mind that something else interesting will always come along. If you have misgivings, simply put away your checkbook and go back to watching the classifieds.

The restoration of special-interest automobiles is a huge, many-sided topic. However, there are common pitfalls, even for the experienced, and I'll try to warn you of those.

To begin with, before undertaking a major project on any car, sit down and make an honest projection of all the costs involved. If the Alfa in question is rare or special, or simply has strong senti-

Club concours events bring out beautiful examples of rare Alfas, and give everyone incentive to put their cars in ultra-clean condition. Author photo.

mental value, you may well decide the expense to be justifiable or recoverable. Don't make the all-too-typical mistake of pouring lots of money and time into a common model that will never appreciate just because you happen to own it and it needs work. In such cases, you're much further ahead to give someone else the car at a bargain price and simply buy another one in good condition.

Keep in mind this very obvious but frequently overlooked fact—it costs no more to restore a really desirable, interesting Alfa than it does to fix a plain one in comparable shape. The interesting Alfa will return your investment, the plain one will simply be an expense.

For the do-it-yourselfers, here are a few pointers learned the hard way. First, don't attempt major body and mechanical projects on the same car simultaneously. Avoid a major restoration project on more than one car at a time, no matter how tempting or logical it may seem. Finally, acquire as many parts as possible in advance of a teardown.

For those having the work done for them, the most important factor is to agree on the extent of repair, expected quality level and the cost before the work is actually started. Keep your restorer well informed of how you plan to use the car. Discuss the unexpected, such as concealed rust, how it should be handled, and the effect on the estimate. Be sure you are both really speaking the same language. While it is disappointing to have a car come out poorer than desired, show-quality work is also unnecessarily expensive for a car that will see daily use.

Restoring an Alfa can be a very relaxing and educational hobby for those who enjoy such activities. The reward is particularly sweet when your efforts bring a concours trophy, or when you go out to the garage just to admire the prize you brought back to usefulness.

The joys of Alfa ownership, or of any hobby for that matter, can be greatly enhanced by association with other people who share your interest and enthusiasm. The Alfa Romeo Owners Club, or AROC, was founded in the Chicago area for just that reason back in 1958 by Bruce Young. The Giuliettas were just beginning to be imported by the Max Hoffman organization then, and the club provided as much of a survival function as it did companionship. Early newsletters are treasure houses of information on Giulietta problems and their solutions.

As the cars became more reliable, the newsletter topics changed from winter starting techniques to performance tips and maintenance procedures. The want-ad section alone is an invaluable source of rare parts and interesting cars, and is worth the cost of membership all by itself.

AROC members compete with every imaginable type of vehicle. Here in the pit lane at Waterford Hills, Alfas spanning over twenty years are lined up for the time trials. Author photo.

The AROC is organized on two distinct levels—there are approximately thirty local chapters with a national organization to tie them together. The primary activities occur on the local level, with events such as autocrosses, picnics, tours, tech sessions, parties and monthly meetings as the typical offerings. The national club provides a blanket insurance policy for events, a monthly magazine called *Alfa Owner*, a standardized set of safety regulations and what has come to be the high point of the year for many owners—the AROC annual meeting.

What began as a legal requirement of incorporation—to meet once a year to elect officers—has grown into a gala four-day event that draws people from all across the country. The chapters present competitive bids to host each year's get-together, so the meetings tend to rotate to different regions.

But the members themselves are the club's best feature. A remarkable group, they will at various times help, educate, compete with, entertain and occasionally infuriate you. They will never bore you. They make the club a marvelous phenomenon, a source of as much enjoyment for me as the cars themselves. I have found many wonderful friendships there, and recommend it as a resource that no one interested in Alfa Romeos should overlook.

Joining the Alfa Romeo Owners Club can open the door to technical help, a variety of motorsports activities and many interesting friendships. Applications for membership or further information should be addressed to:

Glenna Garrett
Executive Secretary, AROC
2304 San Pasqual Valley Road
Escondido, CA 92027
(714) 747-5240

Canadian Alfa owners also have their own national club. Although a newer and smaller organization than the AROC, the enthusiasm level of their membership more than compensates. Contact them at:

Alfa Romeo Club of Canada
P.O. Box 62, Station Q
Toronto, Ontario M4T2L7
Canada

ALFAS AS INVESTMENTS

Financial advisors tend to classify special-interest automobiles as risky and poor investments, and recommend against them. Enthusiasts, on the other hand, generally regard cars as spectacular investments, having seen many exotics appreciate dramatically, particularly through the seventies. It would be easy to dismiss either viewpoint as overly biased—the financial people toward the conventional stock and bond transactions, and the enthusiasts toward their beloved cars. Which group should you believe? It all depends on how realistic you want to be.

The factor that reconciles these two divergent outlooks is the personal time that typically must be expended on an automobile. Frequently, a sale that appears highly favorable for a lucky owner seems less so when it is put in terms of an hourly rate for all his careful maintenance and restoration efforts. In most cases, it would have proven more profitable to have simply put the money in the bank and then spent those extra hours working at a minimum-wage job. The financial types take such things into account in their negative appraisals, while the enthusiasts tend to regard any time spent on their cars as part of the actual return. Once you realize this, it becomes possible to enjoy automobile collecting for what it really is—a hobby that can pay for itself or better, while providing educational and social opportunities.

And if you should happen to make money on a car, there are also some very nice tax advantages to consider. For instance, all the expenses that went into maintaining or improving the car are deductible, so all receipts should be kept for documentation. Also, cars are usually held long enough for any profits to be taxed at the very favorable capital-gains rate, and there is no tax consideration at all on any appreciation unless you actually sell.

Automobiles also have the usual advantage of real investments over paper holdings—the owner can exert a significant influence on their value. Just as painting and landscaping can help sell a house, the cosmetic and mechanical condition of a car will obviously affect its selling price. If your stock goes down, well, that's too bad. But if your exotic isn't selling, a tune-up, some polish and a little creative marketing can work wonders.

When it comes to Alfa Romeos, or any good sports car, there is the added advantage of emotional appeal. After all—isn't that why you became interested in the first place? Seeing and hearing these cars in action as their owners enjoy them cannot be overrated as a major contributor to their desirability. That's why simply storing a car and waiting for it to appreciate can be self-defeating—it's very bad advertising.

What models offer the best return? Obviously any rare or special-bodied Alfa should have excellent potential, with the higher-performance versions having a definite edge. The trick is to acquire a model that is still undervalued, before other collectors begin to realize its desirability. However, the regular production models should not be overlooked as collectables. They frequently rebound in value after the initial depreciation, as normal attrition thins their numbers and people begin looking for well-preserved examples. This is particularly true after a popular model has been discontinued.

The best approach is to regard the purchase of an Alfa, or any automobile, as not purely a financial investment. Rather, learn about the cars and see if they truly interest you. Only buy one you really want to own and use, one you wouldn't mind being stuck with should its resale value drop instead of rise. The best risks are the models that really stir your desires, for they will most likely have the same effect on others.

Keep in mind that lower-priced cars have a larger pool of potential buyers. Also, the upper limit of any model's appreciation will be determined by the willingness and ability of prospective owners to pay. Finally, a rapidly increasing price cannot be counted on to continue indefinitely, and generally flattens out at the level deemed fair by the market.

Many enthusiasts have mixed feelings about the rise in value of exotics and their increasing usage as investments. They fear the cars will eventually become priced out of their reach. Actually, a moderate level of appreciation can be beneficial, helping the owner justify the maintenance and restoration costs of a special vehicle. For the very rare and desirable cars, high appreciation allows their preservation in museum-quality condition for us all to enjoy.

With only a few exceptions, Alfa Romeos tend to fall into the moderate appreciation category —they are the kind of car you buy to use and enjoy, not to make a financial killing. Approach them on this basis, and they will always be enjoyable experiences. Take good care of your Alfa, and its inherent desirability will be your best assurance of a reasonable return.

Establishing an investment rating system is one of those hazardous undertakings that could easily result in many unhappy owners after my scalp. So let me start with a reminder that investment ratings have very little to do with the desirability of an Alfa as an automobile. In fact, by their very nature, ratings are biased against the current or recent models, which typically will undergo some initial depreciation and as such are not really investments.

Besides, very few Alfas are ever purchased purely or even primarily for financial gain. They're real, everyday usable cars that can make routine driving a genuine delight. While some models have proven economically advantageous to their owners, the high inflation of the seventies plus skyrocketing new-car prices were primarily to blame for the rapid appreciation of most exotic vehicles. And, in retrospect, many of the models that appreciated so quickly were terribly underpriced and real bargains to begin with. There is also no guarantee the trend will continue.

This is no more than an attempt to provide some relative investment ranking of the various Alfa models for those new to the marque. It is sometimes difficult to separate past performance from future expectations, or to keep the essential desirability of the more coveted and rare Alfas from influencing their rating. If nothing else, the ratings should provoke many hours of argument and discussion at Alfa club meetings.

The thinking behind the various rankings is as follows:

★Production Alfa, no investment value but may be excellent, bargain-priced used car.

★★Production Alfa, offers chance of moderate to good appreciation. The best choice for a usable, everyday exotic sport car.

★★★Special interest Alfa, but only slight appreciation likely. An affordable collector car.

★★★★Special interest Alfa, exciting to look at or drive, good appreciation possible and likely. Every enthusiast should have one of these.

★★★★★The rarest and most desirable variety of special interest Alfa, the stuff of legends. This superb class of vehicle transcends mere investment ratings.

1986 Update

Since this Buyer's Guide was first written in 1983, a number of events have occurred, the most significant being the passage of the income tax reform bill of 1986. The elimination of the special treatment for capital gains particularly affects car collectors, as does the loss of the state sales tax deduction on automobiles. These changes make it much more important to keep good records of all expenses relating to a specialty car you expect to appreciate, so the true cost can be documented.

These new regulations will probably also encourage enthusiasts to trade their specialty vehicles, rather than sell them, as a way of postponing any taxable gain. Look for enterprising services and magazines to appear that will help prospective traders find each other.

Remember, nothing is permanent about the new tax rules, either. Other equally drastic revisions are possible in the future.

The wild appreciation that affected all collector cars in the late seventies slowed, and prices remained flat through the early eighties as the inflation rate dropped. They seem to be climbing again, but in a more selective and predictable manner. The price gap seems to be widening between the really desirable Alfas and the higher-volume production models.

And there seems to be a cascade effect—as a particular model's price goes up out of sight, collectors seem to then be turning to the next most desirable vehicle, thereby pulling its price up as well. The GTZ offers a good example: As asking prices approach $80,000, attention turned to the previously overlooked GTA (its price climbed into the twenties as a result). Realizing this was happening, many enthusiasts are acquiring their special-interest Alfa now while they can still afford one—and plan to keep it for a long time. This will also have a raising effect on prices as cars are taken out of circulation.

The lesson here is fairly clear: If there is a special-interest Alfa you've always intended to buy and it's still in your price range, don't wait much longer or you may miss your chance forever.

The 6C-2500 was not a postwar Alfa in the strict sense. It was first produced in 1939 as a five-place Berlina, or sedan, with many interesting coupe and roadster adaptations. As with most other automotive firms, resuming production of prewar offerings was the key to Alfa's remaining in the car business and retaining its skilled labor force.

The 6C-2500 served well in that function, providing the much-needed breathing space for new designs to be generated and bombed-out plants to be rebuilt. The series was reborn in 1947 as the Freccia d'Oro, or "Golden Arrow," a five-place touring car. Coupe and cabriolet versions quickly followed with bodies by Farina, Touring, Ghia and others. Production of the 6C-2500 finally ended in 1953, when thirty-four cars were built.

In its day, the 2500 was very representative of the more traditional, or vintage, Alfa approach to motoring. It was fairly large, expensive and fast. As the last Alfa with a separate frame, the coach-builders found it to be an adaptable and respected platform for practicing their skills, and many variations appeared. The emphasis, as always, was on a sporting, race-derived engine and chassis. Technical refinements included a high-rpm, twin-cam, six-cylinder engine, fully independent suspension and rear torsion bar springing.

The wealthy and the famous bought these Alfas and enjoyed them for their status value as well as their driving characteristics. They were quite soft riding, light steering and more nimble than their bulk would suggest. The 2500's were aimed at the same market then as the Maserati Quattro-porte was in the mid-sixties.

Because the 2500 straddled two distinct automotive periods, it is hard to categorize and its value as a collector car suffered for a long time as a result. With its envelope body, it is definitely not vintage in the sense of the thirties Alfas, nor would one ever be mistaken for any of the "modern" designs. The 6C-2500 is a real value for the enthusiast seeking an interesting yet reasonably priced older Alfa. A genuine find would be one of the three 6C-2500 Competizione, or competition, coupes that were built in 1950.

Because these cars have been out of production over thirty years, parts are not readily available. Also, with few exceptions, the 6C-2500's are right-hand-drive. Offsetting these disadvantages is an active and enthusiastic 6C-2500 registry, and any owner or potential owner would be well advised to join. The sharing of technical assistance, spares and interesting contacts will greatly enhance the enjoyment of 6C-2500 ownership.

Nort Newman's beautiful 6C-2500 Farina-bodied cabriolet had at one time been reduced to a parts-car and was languishing in a salvage yard. Nort rescued and restored it to its present like-new state, and shows it frequently at Southern California concours. With top down, one suddenly realizes this is a four-place car. By more recent Alfa standards, these vehicles are really quite large. Note how the door structure extends down into the rocker panel area. Author photo.

A rare left-hand-drive model. The steering mechanical pieces are easily switched from side to side, but the instrument panel and floorpan must also be changed. Don Bruno photo.

The soft, rounded lines concluded very logically and unobtrusively at the car's rear. Author photo.

A Super Sport Pininfarina cabriolet with "nerf-bar" to ward off the careless. Tom Tann photo.

The 6C-2500 instrument panels had a classical elegance that never let the driver forget the vehicle's sporting aspects. Don Bruno photo.

The single Weber carburetor identified the engine as the sport version. Individual cam covers topped the big in-line six. Author photo.

The Super Sport engine came with three dual-throat Webers, each having its own filter canister. The 2500's did not make normal automotive engine sounds when running, but invoked images of precision heavy machinery. Don Bruno photo.

The 6C-2500 Series

ENGINE
Type: In-line six-cylinder
Block: Cast iron
Head: Cast aluminum, cross flow, hemispherical chambers
Bore x stroke: 72mm x 100mm
Displacement: 2443 cc (2500 nominal)
Valve actuation: Gear driven with chain idler, dual overhead cams, bucket tappets with threaded adjustment

DRIVETRAIN
Transmission: Four-speed, synchromesh
Clutch: Single-disc with coil-spring pressure plate, mechanical actuation
Driveshaft: Two-piece with three Metalastic joints, center support bearing
Tire size: 6.50 x 17
Wheels: 17-inch rim

SUSPENSION
Front: Upper and lower links with double trailing arms, coil springs, king pins
Rear: Swing axles with longitudinal torsion bars
Shock absorbers: Tubular, hydraulic

The heart-shaped grille that has become a distinctive Alfa trademark was a diminutive reminder of the large and beautiful external radiator shells on the vintage cars. Successive Alfa models have had progressively smaller grilles as styling and aerodynamics have dictated lower front ends, and grille size can almost be used to date an unknown Alfa model. Don Bruno photo.

A "mystery" 2500 belonging to Bob Tucker that defied attempts at identification for many years. It was eventually discovered to be a one-off commissioned by Giovanni Lurani with lightweight tubular chassis by Cattaneo and body by Riva. Bob Schnittger photo.

Alfas have always had the benefit of huge brakes. The drums of the 6C-2500's took good advantage of the space provided by the 17- and 18-inch rims that were used. Don Bruno photo.

The Freccia d'Oro was Alfa's first postwar effort on the 6C-2500 chassis. The average Alfa owner is usually stunned by the sheer physical size of this car. Its long wheelbase of 118 inches contributed both to the appearance of length and the excellent ride. Author photo.

CHAPTER 2
1900 SERIES

As Alfa's first postwar design, the 1900 was considered a lightweight compact model at its introduction in 1950. Its four-cylinder engine continued the twin-cam tradition, but featured a one-piece cast-iron block and aluminum head. The state-of-tune varied from ninety to 115 horsepower depending on the application.

This was the last Alfa model to utilize the company's classical valve-adjusting mechanism. The valve spring retainer was a two-piece unit, with matching serrated faces. The upper part screwed onto the threaded valve stem and rotated to provide the desired cam clearance. The serrations then locked in the setting. Routine adjustment was achieved with a special tool similar to a drill-chuck key which compressed the valve spring enough to separate the serrations. A hefty screwdriver was often substituted, with less finesse but equivalent results. The disadvantage of this system was a relatively high valve-train inertia for an overhead cam drive.

The unit-body construction was not only Alfa's first nonframe design, but the 1900 was its first vehicle intended for mass production. In keeping with the lower cost, a solid rear axle was provided, though it was well located with a triangulating link and radius arms. Double wishbone suspension arms were used in front. Huge, finned-aluminum drum brakes were utilized to complete the sporting character.

By today's grand touring standards, the 1900 cars are somewhat stodgy and trucklike to drive. This had kept prices quite low and, until fairly recently, it was not unusual to find good examples for giveaway prices. Increasing scarcity and a growing appreciation of this sturdy model have eliminated such bargains, but the 1900 remains a good value for collectors seeking an interesting car. Many mechanical and hydraulic parts are still available as they were carried over into later vehicles, particularly the "old" 2000, 2600 and Giulietta.

The models consisted mainly of sedans and coupes, although a handful of roadsters were made. The sedans generally had steel bodies and the coupes aluminum. Coupes were commonly referred to as "three-window" or "five-window" depending on the side-glass configuration. It's poor arithmetic, but that's tradition for you. Earlier coupes usually had smaller rear windows and side doors that wrapped down around the rocker panel area, a carryover from the 6C-2500; while the later ones had larger rear windows and doors that stopped above the rocker in the more modern fashion.

Most 1900 owners I talked to looked puzzled and shrugged when asked about problem areas, and indicated their cars were quite trouble-free. More than anything, this may reflect today's usage of the 1900 as primarily a collector vehicle rather than an everyday car. Actually, they are mechanically quite sound, with water-pump bearings, second-gear synchros and seized brake pistons the main items to watch for.

Corrosion is a major concern on the aluminum-bodied cars, particularly around door and rocker edges and in the wheelwell arches, areas where the aluminum skin wraps around steel framing. Restoration of perforated aluminum requires a much higher skill level than rust repair of steel, and is more expensive as a result. Also inspect for floorpan rust, especially around the rear suspension linkage attachment points.

One last pitfall involves the wool and mohair interiors used on many 1900's—mothballs will become a new and effective addition to your toolbox if you acquire one of these chunky Alfas.

All Body Styles ★★★★

CHASSIS NUMBERS	
1950-1954:	1900.00001-1900.09999——Berlina
1952:	1900.01331-1900.01539——T.I./T.I. Super/Super
1953-1955:	1900TI.04786-1900TI.15700
1951-1958:	1900C.00051-1900C.10600——Sprint/Super Sprint
1952:	1900L.00071-1900L.01100——Cabriolet

This lovely five-window Touring-bodied coupe shows off its lines even better without the bumpers. The Giulietta's styling was obviously influenced by the front-end appearance of this model. Jeanette Benson photo.

The 1900 Series

ENGINE
Type: In-line four-cylinder
Block: Cast iron
Head: Cast aluminum, cross flow, hemispherical chambers
Bore x stroke: 82.55mm x 88mm
Displacement: 1884 cc (1900 nominal)
Valve actuation: Chain driven, dual overhead cams, bucket tappets with threaded adjustment
DRIVETRAIN
Transmission: Four- or five-speed, synchromesh
Clutch: Single-disc with coil-spring pressure plate, mechanical actuation
Driveshaft: Two-piece with double front Metalastic joints, rear U-joint
Tire size: 6.00 x 16 or 165 x 400
Wheels: 16-inch or 400 mm rim
SUSPENSION
Front: Double A-arm, sway bar, coil springs, kingpins
Rear: Solid axle with longitudinal radius arms and triangular lateral locator, coil springs
Shock absorbers: Tubular, hydraulic

The 1900 engine featured a distributor driven off the rear of the exhaust cam, and a tricky bit of casting work to provide a "tunnel" for the front cam drive chain. Two dual-throat, downdraft Solex carbs under the air plenum identify this engine as the Super Sport version. Author photo.

Dave Yager's Touring-bodied three-window coupe leaves little doubt as to the Giulietta Spider's styling origins. Author photo.

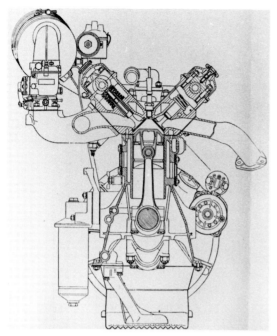

The sturdy 1900 engine offered a blend of new and old features. Factory artwork.

The deeply sculptured tail displays the Touring's familiar winged coachbuilder insignia. The rear window size and door ending above the rocker mark this as a later 1900, while the license plate warns the knowledgeable that it is the highest-performance, 115-horsepower Super Sport version. Jeanette Benson photo.

The front suspension consisted of double A-arms and coil springs. The very long lower control arms gave very good camber change characteristics. Factory artwork.

The 1900's were beautifully instrumented with a delightful array of gauges, toggles and lights to amuse the driver. Don Bruno photo.

A three-window coupe by Ghia with wide and heavily-styled C-pillar. Dave Yager photo.

Boano achieved an excellent highlighting of the traditional Alfa grille on this 1900, but treatment of the rear was not as pleasing as the styling of the front would lead one to expect. Bob Schnittger photos.

Little did anyone, Alfa Romeo included, suspect the incredible success and acceptance awaiting the Giulietta when it was introduced in 1954. When originally announced as a prize in a government lottery, the design was only in an early prototype stage. The ongoing delays in delivery caused much unhappiness and bordered on scandal.

When the first Giulietta Sprints were finally handed over to their fortunate owners, word of their excellence spread quickly. Demand caused production goals to be dramatically increased many times. The Giulietta literally established Alfa Romeo and Bertone, the coachbuilder, as high-volume manufacturers. An excellent and entertaining account of this portion of Alfa history can be found in the December 1964 *Road & Track.*

The Sprint coupe was soon followed by the Giulietta Berlina, or four-door sedan. By the summer of 1955, a Spider, or roadster version, was announced with body by Pininfarina. To satisfy the clamoring for even more performance and improve the Giulietta's success in competition, Veloce versions of both Sprint and Spider were announced in 1956. Despite only a small advertised horsepower increase, the Veloces were much faster.

The differences came from higher compression, hotter cams, twin Weber carbs to replace the single Solex, tubular headers and a finned cast-aluminum sump featuring a built-in oil cooler and surge baffles to keep it all cool. But power wasn't everything, and the single-carb or Normale versions still attracted enthusiasts who felt the less cluttered engine provided lighter steering, more neutral handling and a flatter torque curve.

The same factors that made the Giulietta so popular in the fifties are still valid today. The high state-of-tune, excellent handling and ride, and astounding brakes still delight the enthusiast. They have that elusive feel of quality and substance all too often lacking in small, light vehicles.

A Giulietta has almost the same driving feel as the more recent models. In that sense, it is the first of the older, collectable Alfas to offer a nonvintage character. To the seat of the pants, the 1300-cc engine seems virtually torqueless, particularly the Veloce. Fast starts require high rpm and lots of clutch slippage. Yet the acceleration figures often match or exceed the later 1750 and 2000 models which subjectively would be judged much faster. For example, *Road & Track* timed a 1958 Spider Veloce through the quarter-mile in 17.6 seconds, a respectable acceleration for any of the four-cylinder Alfas.

Problem areas include short water-pump bearing life and a slight tendency to burn exhaust valves. Giuliettas exhibit considerable piston slap when cold, but it is of no consequence. The Giulietta also has a reputation for unreliable electrics that is misleading and somewhat undeserved. The components themselves are satisfactory—most of the trouble originates from the wiring system. Weak fuse clips, easily corroded fuse ends, screwpost wire terminations, a rear-mounted battery and the use of wax-impregnated cloth covering on the wires instead of vinyl plastic are the primary culprits. Running a heavy-gauge ground strap from the battery to the engine block was a common and effective improvement.

Corrosion areas to be wary of include the rocker panel box structures, brake lines and the rear-suspension radius-arm attachment points. The rear axle can tear loose from the body if the metal at these attachment points becomes sufficiently weakened by rust.

The Veloce models have their own unique difficulties traceable to higher performance. These are higher octane requirements, a tendency to foul plugs in city driving, and the need to keep the dual Weber carbs synchronized and idle-balanced. They will barely tolerate modern unleaded premium fuels, and in severe cases the ignition timing should be retarded to prevent detonation. If not always driven hard, a Veloce engine will load up and the spark plugs foul. Frequent plug changes are recommended and necessary to keep them running well. The Veloce's aluminum oil-cooler sump is so effective that oil temperature only registers on the gauge under racing conditions. In cold weather, this

Berlina ★★★
Sprint ★★★
Sprint Veloce ★★★
Spider ★★★
Spider Veloce ★★★★

CHASSIS NUMBERS
1955-1960: 1488.00002-1488.35200——Berlina
1954-1959: 1493.00011-1493.10301——Sprint/Sprint Veloce
1955-1959: 1495.00016-1495.07213——Spider/Spider Veloce

Barry Frantz's absolutely immaculate 1956 750-Series Giulietta Berlina with over 175,000 kilometers on the odometer. Author photo.

prevents even the coolant from reaching full temperature and makes the heater somewhat academic. Combined with a soft top that did not seal well above the side windows, the 1300 Spider Veloce was not an ideal winter vehicle.

Parts are somewhat more difficult to obtain for these early Giuliettas, as the early components were soon upgraded with the 101 Series to improve durability. Most of the changes are not immediately obvious, such as valve stem size and steering idler bushing diameter. Road abrasion and rust also take their toll on the Veloce headers, and replacements are becoming increasingly difficult to find.

Other changes were more sweeping, such as the complete reworking of the transmission to a split-case design that allowed adding a fifth gear. At that time, the strut-type synchronizers were dropped in favor of the Porsche design which is still used in Alfa's present models. The Weber carbs were also updated on the 101 Series to provide bearings instead of bushings on the throttle shafts and eliminate a wear problem.

Because of this situation, the 750-Series vehicles should be considered to have minimal parts interchangeability with later Giuliettas. Yet there is still a reasonable supply of 750 parts-cars, and most routine maintenance items are still commercially available.

Why consider a 750-Series Giulietta? Many Alfa enthusiasts prefer them to the later 1300's for their unique character and feel. The engines have a freer-revving response and their appearance is somewhat lighter and more graceful. This is particularly true of the Spider; its original short-wheelbase, small-taillight configuration is commonly considered the most interesting and desirable. The bodies on these early cars were also individually hand-fabricated, adding another element of appeal. The 750-Series Giulietta was really the first of the modern Alfas, and the basis for most of what was to follow.

Berlina

Shortly after the debut of the Giulietta Sprint, the sedan version, or Berlina, appeared. It was to be the most popular of the Giulietta series, with 24,929 produced by 1959. These cars saw duty in Italy and the rest of Europe in a wide variety of nonsporting applications, from police cars and taxicabs to everyday family transportation. As such, they were simply part of a long and continuing tradition at Alfa of providing a quality sedan based on its more sporting components. American enthusiasts are usually boggled to discover that such beautiful aluminum twin-cam engines are being "wasted" on cabs; but perhaps that at least helps to explain the worldwide notoriety of Italian taxi drivers.

The lines of the Giulietta Berlina can best be described as ugly-duckling cute, and it is saved from harsher judgments only by its small size. Most Alfa sedans are similar in that they are almost deliberately nonstyled, perhaps to not distract from judging them on the merits of their fine machinery. It's an unusual practice for a manufacturer, and shows an amazing level of self-confidence.

Subjected to American tastes, the Giulietta Berlina usually provokes pointing and smiles and occasional giggles. Critics and Alfa enthusiasts alike, however, are usually quite amazed by their first ride in one. There is an astonishing level of comfort and space for four people in the interior, and the excellent ride qualities of the Giulietta chassis seem even more refined than in the sporting models.

Very few Giulietta Berlinas of either the 750 or 101 Series were brought to the U.S., and they are very hard to find, particularly in good condition. Prices range from please-tow-it-away to quite expensive, depending on the condition of the car and its worth in the eyes of its owner. If you really want one of these early sedans, the best approach may be to find one in Europe where they were far more available. The price should be quite reasonable there, and because they are pre-1968 vehicles, they can be brought to America with a minimum of bureaucratic foolishness.

The Giulietta Berlina is a perfect example of a speculation vehicle: Since it has no solid price basis in the U.S., bargains are still possible. And there are Alfa collectors who will pay a fairly good price after being tempted by a good example of one.

Sprint/Sprint Veloce

History buffs who appreciate cars of genuine significance have much to admire in the Giulietta Sprint. It is hard to imagine Alfa Romeo becoming the volume producer it is today without the impetus of the Giulietta and all its derivations. Thus the Sprint, as the first Giulietta, was truly a pivotal car for Alfa, to the extent that it would actually be more logical to refer to pre- and post-Giulietta periods rather than pre- and postwar models.

It is easy to get the impression that Alfa was just a bit nervous about the launch of its new small car back in 1954. Even the Giulietta designation, a playful Shakespearean pun with the company's name, seemed to indicate a less-than-serious approach. It almost provided the "out" of saying it was all just in fun if the car were to be a failure.

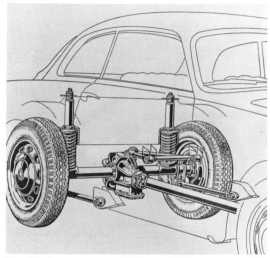

The Giulietta rear suspension was straightforward and effective. Two radius arms and a triangulating link kept the solid rear axle well-located, and coil springs provided support. The cast aluminum differential housing was well-ribbed for both strength and cooling. Factory artwork.

Instrumentation was quite stark, giving only speed, oil pressure and fuel level. A four-speed column shift operated through a cable linkage system to the transmission. Some of the early Sprints also had this feature. Author photo.

MODEL: Giulietta Berlina
BODY TYPE: four-door sedan
BODY DESIGNER: factory
WHEELBASE 93.7 in.
TRACK, FRONT: 50.9 in.
        REAR: 50.0 in.
WEIGHT: 2013 lbs.
BRAKES, FRONT: Alfin drum
        REAR: Alfin drum
COMPRESSION RATIO: 7.5:1
CARBURETION: single downdraft Solex
HORSEPOWER: 53 @ 5500 rpm
AXLE RATIO: 9/41 (4.56)

The engine bay was simplicity itself. Several unique features were a cam-driven fuel pump on the front of the head and a manually engaged starter motor. The miniscule carburetor was serviceable if not inspiring. There was such good hood clearance that the extra height of the later four-cylinder engines could easily be accommodated, and there have been at least several 2000-cc conversions. Author photo.

There was good reason to worry, for the Giulietta Sprint did not fit any proven, comfortable sales niche. Being unique for its time, it had to stand on its own merits and create its own market. It did that quite well, and in the process helped define the emerging concept of the small grand touring car.

Despite sharing the same mechanicals and state-of-tune with the Spider, the Sprints had a decidedly mellower personality. The slightly larger size and weight, the longer wheelbase, the better soundproofing and the more padded and luxurious interior of the Sprint created a much softer and smoother driving impression than the Spartan roadster. There was sufficient difference that Spider owners were frequently surprised and mildly disappointed by their first drive in a Sprint.

This disparity in character provides a real choice between sports and touring applications. Now that the Giuliettas are approaching collector status, there is much less need for the long-distance comfort of the Sprint, possibly explaining why its asking prices have not paced those of the Spiders, particularly the Veloce.

Yet, the Sprint has the edge in the history books, and this could eventually offset the emotional appeal of the open cars. The irony is that the Sprint was originally the more expensive model. Meanwhile, the 750 Sprints offer a very good bargain as well as a potentially good investment.

Spider/Spider Veloce

The Giulietta Spider must have been quite a shock to the other manufacturers of small sports cars when it was first released to the public. Suddenly, there was a new state-of-the-art. With its roll-up windows, excellent ride and delightfully simple top mechanism, the Spider made almost all the other sporting vehicles of 1955 look terribly dated. No longer was it necessary to be masochistic or wear a kidney belt to have fun driving. Pininfarina's seamless, tight-fitting coachwork wrapped the Spider's advanced mechanicals in a classic and attractive style without any detracting gimmickry.

Occasionally cars come along that look great on paper and disappoint when driven. Not so the Giulietta. Many of the early Spider owners raced their cars—it was much easier to do then—and gave their competitors many painful lessons in the advantages of a twin-cam engine, huge brakes and a modern chassis.

Today, the 750 Spiders are the most rapidly appreciating of the production Giuliettas, with the Weber-carbureted Veloce model commanding the highest prices. Condition is very important in determining price on the 750 Spiders. Rusty ones can still be had for several hundred dollars, while really excellent examples are now priced in the same range as the new Spiders.

It may be necessary to actually drive one of these cars to understand what all the fuss is about. Discussion about all its modern attributes and good performance is really inadequate compared to a first-hand experience. *Road & Track* was so impressed, it concluded, "A car has no business being so desirable."

The initial surprise will be the high state-of-tune—the emission laws have simply eliminated performance engines like the Giulietta's from America's recent experience. A Veloce will feel out of tune and weak up to 3500 rpm, come to life and wind strongly to 5000, and then *really* go, right on up to 8000.

To do this, it is necessary to completely ignore the 6700 rpm redline on the tach. Most Giulietta owners soon discover this, and keep their 1300's wound up mercilessly. The penalties are an occasional broken valve spring and somewhat shortened piston ring life, but little else. With their less-effective breathing, there's not as much reason to push a Normale over 7000 rpm, especially since all the engine components are not as heavy-duty as on the Veloce.

The short wheelbase and excellent shock absorber characteristics allow the 750 Spiders to simply track over swells and dips in the road, following the contour, instead of exhibiting the more typical separate front and rear bobbing motions of larger cars. Giuliettas will transcend obstacles such as rough railroad tracks with rapid wheel motions, transmitting a minimum amount of jolt to the driver with no loss of directional stability. They are close to the ideal of the inert platform that isolates the driver from the road surface while optimizing his utilization of it. The stock Girling shock absorbers on the Giuliettas have a lot to do with the excellent road manners, and I recommend them over any aftermarket units; their valving is near-perfect.

Cars such as the Giulietta Spider tend to provoke, encourage and reward hard driving. Fortunately, like all Alfas, they are extremely forgiving cars with response characteristics that allow the most amateur of drivers to look and feel like an expert.

Cornered past their limit, they go into a mild understeer that is easily counteracted. Even the most panicky of reactions—jumping off the gas or hitting the brakes—simply scrubs off enough speed

Engine compartment of a Giulietta Sprint Veloce. Both Spider and Sprint Veloces used the distinctive air-filter box strapped to the firewall. The air inlet hose shared a common scoop under the left headlight with the cool-air ductwork that supplied a vent by the driver's feet. When the vent was opened, the induction sounds of the Webers filled the interior—great for spirited driving but tiresome on a long trip. Author photo.

The 750 Giulietta Sprint had the same stamped grille and the same type eyebrows as the 750 Spider, which is the quickest way to distinguish the early model. The precision fit of the doors, hood and trunk lid to the body was one of the benefits of the hand-fabrication techniques employed. Author photo.

to bring them back under control. Giulietta Spiders always seem to provide multiple opportunities to recover from silly situations. High-speed emergency maneuvers are accomplished without any great fuss.

Body corrosion is the primary item to watch out for, and is the largest single factor separating the expensive cars from the giveaways. Because they were hand-fabricated, the sheetmetal tended to be a heavier gauge to allow filing and grinding, and was more ductile to permit easier forming. The particular alloy used seemed to be somewhat more rust-resistant than some of the more modern formulations, and the extra thickness bought more time before holes appeared. Offsetting this was the lack of sealants and anticorrosion coatings that were routinely used on high-production vehicles. In particular, there is some question whether enclosed regions such as the rocker panels received any protective coating at all, even paint.

The Spiders, even the later ones, should always be inspected for interior rust as well. No soft top seals perfectly or is always up when the rain starts to fall, and the mats will trap and hide the water while it rusts the car from the inside. Be sure to check behind and under the seats, in the footwells and then inspect the entire floorpan from underneath.

Despite their small size, the Giulietta Spiders are quite comfortable, even for the tall driver. The legroom, in fact, is noticeably more generous than in today's somewhat larger Spider.

Even if you never plan to own a Giulietta Spider, you should at least arrange for a ride or drive in one just to round out your automotive experience. It will really change your perspective on where the last quarter-century's progress has taken us.

What might have been . . . Bertone was greatly influenced by his own Arnolt Bristol design when he made this one-off prototype for the Giulietta Spider. This car is surprisingly quick thanks to its very light weight, but also somewhat flexible. While it is unquestionably cute, Alfa undoubtedly made the correct choice from the standpoint of having an enduring, classic style by instead going with Pininfarina's concept. The very existence of this car was not known until it appeared in *The New York Times* for $1,500 in the mid-seventies, and over forty people passed up the opportunity to own this gem, thinking it was just someone's customized Giulietta. Author photos.

MODEL: 750-Series Giulietta Sprint, Sprint Veloce
BODY TYPE: two-door coupe
BODY DESIGNER: Bertone
WHEELBASE 93.7 in.
TRACK, FRONT: 50.9 in.
        REAR: 50.0 in.
WEIGHT: 1936 lbs., Sprint; 1969 lbs., Sprint Veloce
BRAKES, FRONT: Alfin drum
        REAR: Alfin drum
COMPRESSION RATIO: 8.5:1, Sprint; 9.1:1, Sprint Veloce
CARBURETION: single downdraft Solex, Sprint; dual sidedraft
    Webers, Sprint Veloce
HORSEPOWER: 80 @ 6300 rpm, Sprint; 90 @ 6500 rpm, Sprint
    Veloce
AXLE RATIO: 9/41 (4.56), Sprint
            10/41 (4.1), Sprint Veloce

Bertone and the Giulietta Sprint—serendipity at its best. Author photo.

From the rear, the heavy casting on the trunk lid and small taillights also said 750. A few of the Sprints also shared taillights with the 750 Spider. In general, the larger the taillights, the later the Spider or Sprint. Author photo.

750-Series Giulietta

ENGINE

Type: In-line four-cylinder
Block: Cast aluminum with slip-fit wet iron liners
Head: Cast aluminum, cross flow, hemispherical chambers
Bore x stroke: 74mm x 75mm
Displacement: 1290 cc (1300 nominal)
Valve actuation: Chain driven, dual overhead cams, bucket tappets, shim adjustment

DRIVETRAIN

Transmission: Four-speed, strut-type synchromesh, aluminum tunnel case
Clutch: Single-disc with coil-spring pressure plate, mechanical actuation
Driveshaft: Two-piece with front Metalastic joint, double U-joint, slip spline and center support bearing
Tire size: 155-15
Wheels: 4 1/2 x 15

SUSPENSION

Front: Double A-arm, ball joints, sway bar
Rear: Solid axle with longitudinal radius arms and triangular lateral locator
Shock absorbers: Tubular, hydraulic

A 750-Series Spider in as nice and original condition as can be found. Spotless California cars such as this send Midwesterners away sadly shaking their heads and muttering to themselves about all the lost battles with the salt truck. Jeanette Benson photo.

The 7000 rpm tach and 120 mph speedometer were supplied on the Giulietta Normales. The early 1300's had no glovebox door. Jeanette Benson photo.

The superb front drum brakes of the Giulietta were cast aluminum with iron inserts. The fins provided extra cooling as well as resistance to mechanical distortion. Note the beautiful cast aluminum brake shoes and compare them to the stamped, flimsy sheetmetal shoes in common usage on other cars. "DESTRO" indicated the drum was for use on the right side of the car; "SINESTRA" was cast on the left-side units. Author photo.

The single Solex carburetor and four-into-one cast header of the Normale version. Author photo.

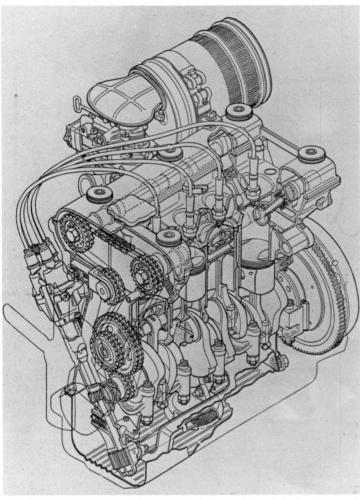

A side cutaway shows the fully counterbalanced crankshaft supported by five main bearings. The hemispherical combustion chambers provided an optimum flame-front, and dual-overhead camshafts allowed the high rpm for which the Giulietta was noted. Factory artwork.

This version of the Alfa badge was used from 1950 to 1960 and was a genuine cloisonne emblem. The red cross on a white background is the flag of the City of Milan, the home of Alfa Romeo. The serpent devouring a man is the crest of the Visconti family of Milan, and dates back to its participation in the Crusades. The surrounding laurel wreath was added in the 1920's to commemorate the company's competition victories. Author photo.

MODEL: 750-Series Giulietta Spider, Spider Veloce
BODY TYPE: two-place roadster
BODY DESIGNER: Pininfarina
WHEELBASE 86.6 in.
TRACK, FRONT: 50.0 in.
     REAR: 50.0 in.
WEIGHT: 1892 lbs., Spider; 1903 lbs., Spider Veloce
BRAKES, FRONT: Alfin drum
     REAR: Alfin drum
COMPRESSION RATIO: 8.5:1, Spider; 9.1:1, Spider Veloce
CARBURETION: single downdraft Solex, Spider; dual sidedraft Webers, Spider Veloce
HORSEPOWER: 80 @ 6300 rpm, Spider; 90 @ 6500 rpm, Spider Veloce
AXLE RATIO: 9/41 (4.56), Spider;
       10/41 (4.1), Spider Veloce

The small split-oval taillights of the 750-Series Spider were delicately styled and an excellent complement to the lines of the roadster. The trunk was deep and could hold a surprising volume of goods. Jeanette Benson photo.

The 102-Series 2000 vehicles were a replacement for the 1900 line. The Berlina and touring-bodied Spider appeared first in 1958. The Sprint coupe followed somewhat later in 1960, and was Bertone's second major styling effort for Alfa. Its lines were very typical of the work Giugiaro was doing for Bertone in this period, and figured prominently in the Giulia Sprint GT.

This particular series was possibly Alfa's least successful postwar design. Constructed over a five-year period ending in 1962, a total of only 7,089 vehicles was built. The usual full range of Berlina, Spider and Sprint models was offered. The Spider was the most popular with 3,443 constructed—most unusual since the sedans usually had the highest production numbers and were the basis for most Alfa series.

The 102-Series 2000, commonly referred to as the "old" two-liter, showed much Giulietta influence in its engine, particularly the valve train. Some 1900 traces were also evident, such as the iron block, individual cam covers and distributor driven off the rear of the cam. The five-speed transmission was shared with the 101 Giulietta SS and SZ.

This particular series was no doubt intended to maintain an active product line in a larger displacement class than the Giulietta. It was inevitable that it would be compared to the Giulietta, a formidable yardstick for evaluating any car.

The 2000's strengths were great smoothness and relaxed high-speed cruising. Both the engine and chassis developed reputations for durability.

Its main failing was that it was underpowered. A Giulietta, even a Normale, would simply outperform it in almost every aspect and was much more fun to drive. The 2000 was not a car that excited.

There were not many "old" 2000's imported to the U.S., and the Spider was almost exclusively the only model seen here. There are no more than a handful of Sprints—I have seen only one—and only a couple of sedans in the country.

The size and styling of the 2000's were quite pleasing, though, and their body and chassis designs were carried over with very little change into the 2600 Series.

They are far more desirable now as collector vehicles than they ever were as contemporary automobiles. Asking prices are all over the map, with some owners appraising values a lot higher than others. Parts are fairly difficult to find, especially for the engine.

One unique problem occurs at rebuild time—supposedly the specified piston ring-gaps are too tight and cause reduced power output, a long break-in period and occasional seizing. Reportedly, this condition can be corrected by the use of slightly larger-than-specified ring-gaps.

Berlina ★ ★ ★
Sprint ★ ★ ★
Spider ★ ★ ★

CHASSIS NUMBERS		
1958-1962:	10200.00001-10200.02947	——Berlina
1960-1962:	10205.00005-10205.01937	——Sprint
1958-1961:	10204.00004-10204.03463	——Spider

The 2000 Spider was noticeably larger than the Giulietta despite the similarity of styling. Author photo.

```
MODEL: 102-Series 2000 Berlina
BODY TYPE: four-door sedan
BODY DESIGNER: factory
WHEELBASE 107.1 in.
TRACK, FRONT: 55.1 in.
       REAR: 53.9 in.
WEIGHT: 2948 lbs.
BRAKES, FRONT: Alfin drum
        REAR: Alfin drum
COMPRESSION RATIO: 8.25:1
CARBURETION: single downdraft Solex
HORSEPOWER: 105 @ 5300 rpm
AXLE RATIO: 9/43 (4.78)
```

```
MODEL: 102-Series 2000 Sprint
BODY TYPE: two-door coupe
BODY DESIGNER: Bertone
WHEELBASE 101.6 in.
TRACK, FRONT: 55.1 in.
       REAR: 53.9 in.
WEIGHT: 2640 lbs.
BRAKES, FRONT: Alfin drum
        REAR: Alfin drum
COMPRESSION RATIO: 8.5:1
CARBURETION: dual sidedraft Solex
HORSEPOWER: 115 @ 5900 rpm
AXLE RATIO: 9/43 (4.78)
```

```
MODEL: 102-Series 2000 Spider
BODY TYPE: two-place roadster
BODY DESIGNER: Touring
WHEELBASE 98.4 in.
TRACK, FRONT: 55.1 in.
       REAR: 53.9 in.
WEIGHT: 2596 lbs.
BRAKES, FRONT: Alfin drum
        REAR: Alfin drum
COMPRESSION RATIO: 8.5:1
CARBURETION: dual sidedraft Solex
HORSEPOWER: 115 @ 5900 rpm
AXLE RATIO: 9/43 (4.78)
```

Jay Nuxoll's well-preserved 2000 Berlina is a very rare car in the U.S. The large vertical tailfins and lights show obvious American styling influence of the period. Author photo.

The 2000 Spider's front-end appearance was lighter than the 2600 version that followed and was easily identified by the twin-snorkel hood scoop. Carburetors were the troublesome Solex 44 PHH with vacuum-actuated secondaries. Author photo.

102-Series 2000

ENGINE
Type: In-line four-cylinder
Block: Cast iron
Head: Cast aluminum, cross flow, hemispherical chambers
Bore x stroke: 84.5mm x 88mm
Displacement: 1975 cc (2000 nominal)
Valve actuation: Chain driven, dual overhead cams, bucket tappets with shim adjustment

DRIVETRAIN
Transmission: Five-speed, synchromesh
Clutch: Single-disc with coil-spring pressure plate, hydraulic actuation
Driveshaft: Two-piece with front Metalastic joint, double U-joint, slip-spline and center support bearing
Tire size: 165 x 400
Wheels: 400 mm rim

SUSPENSION
Front: Double A-arm, sway bar, coil springs, kingpins
Rear: Solid axle with longitudinal radius arms and triangular lateral locator, coil springs
Shock absorbers: Tubular, hydraulic

This excellent-condition 2000 Spider of Mike Alessandro is a European version with only 18,000 miles on it. Mike Alessandro photo.

CHAPTER 5
101-SERIES GIULIETTA

The special-bodied Giuliettas were used to introduce the 101 designation, with the Sprint Speciale first appearing in 1957 and the Sprint Zagato in 1959. Besides the special coachwork, they had many developmental changes throughout the chassis and drivetrain. These mechanical improvements were incorporated into the regular production models during 1959, which was an important transition year.

Most changes were not immediately obvious by simple inspection—for example, many suspension pivot bushing diameters were increased, valve stems went from 7 to 8 mm and water-pump bearings became sealed assemblies. The Weber carbs were updated from the 40 DCO3 to the 40 DCOE-2, along with simplified throttle linkage and a revised intake manifold.

The split-case transmission used in the SS and SZ was adopted across the board with the 101 Series, although the fifth gear was not included on the regular production Giuliettas. Later, a factory update kit made it possible to convert these early 101 gearboxes to five-speeds.

Porsche-type synchronizers were used in the new transmission instead of the strut-type design of the 750 Series. The split case featured greatly simplified servicing, and the basic design is still used today in the 2000 Spider Veloce.

If you own or are considering a 1959 Giulietta, it is important from a parts standpoint to determine if the car is a 750- or 101-Series model, since both types were manufactured that year. Also, the changeover was not abrupt, and some cars were built with a mix of parts.

Problem areas are not much different than on the 750-Series cars, with most of the real nuisance ones such as the water-pump bearing failures eliminated. There is still a tendency to burn exhaust valves, particularly as the guides begin to wear. This can be completely cured in the 101-Series engines by substituting the more expensive sodium-filled exhaust valves from the 105-Series Giulias, which are dimensionally identical. The worn guides, of course, should also be replaced.

The 101 Giulietta lasted until 1962 when the engine size was increased to 1600 cc and it, as well as the car, was renamed the Giulia. These 101 Giuliettas have much to recommend them, including a high level of parts interchangeability with later models. Their durability and reliability were significantly improved over the 750, and they are, in general, easier cars to live with on an everyday basis.

Sprint/Sprint Veloce

While the change to the 101 Series was primarily to upgrade the Giulietta mechanical components, there were trim changes on the coupe body as well that allowed easy identification. The 101 Sprint's grille and "eyebrows" were completely revised and were no longer like the Spider's. The newer design was a bit heavier and busier looking, but the change did give the coupe a more modern and developed appearance. Larger rear taillights had the same effect at the rear. Script and marker lights also began to appear on the Sprint's previously uncluttered flanks.

It is very difficult to describe the differences in feel between the two series of Giulietta Sprints, for they were in reality the same car. The most accurate statement may be that the ambiance of the Sprint changed in the same direction as the mechanical and cosmetic differences—toward maturity and refinement. The Veloce option was continued for the more sporting driver and for those who loved the raucous sounds and extra performance of the dual Webers and tubing headers.

There does not seem to be any significant price difference between early and late Sprints. They also typically sell for less than a Spider in equivalent condition, another victory of heart over head which demonstrates again the Alfa owner's strong preference for performance over luxury.

Spider/Spider Veloce

Unlike the Sprint, the Spider emerged from the 101 update with a longer wheelbase; the elongated doors were quite apparent from the side view. This change had the usual and predictable effect of providing a better ride and slightly slowing the steering reflexes, characteristics that were hardly desired or necessary for the roadster.

Sprint ★★★
Sprint Veloce ★★★
Spider ★★★
Spider Veloce ★★★

CHASSIS NUMBERS		
1959-1960:	1493.20001-1493.26200——Sprint	
1960-1962:	10102.155001-10102.164108	
1959:	1493.11001-1493.11101——Sprint Veloce	
1960-1962:	10102.155001-10102.156384	
1963-1964:	10102.384001-10102.385571——Sprint 1300	
1959-1960:	1495.08001-1495.11900——Spider	
1960-1962:	10103.167001-10103.173086	
1959:	1495.07501-1495.07612——Spider Veloce	
1960-1962:	10103.167001-10103.173066	

The 101 Sprint was most quickly distinguished from the 750 Series by the busier detailing of the front grille and eyebrows. Tom Tann photo.

In addition, the short-wheelbase 750 Spider was such a coherent and satisfying design, that to simply stretch it lost just a bit of the charm and character. For those who really liked Pininfarina's original concept, the stretched version never looked quite correct and it was a common feeling that they really had it right the first time around.

This somewhat explains why the 750 Spiders now sell for at least double their 101 counterparts, despite the latter's considerably improved reliability and weather protection and somewhat better heater. It's really quite simple—the 101 Spiders were much better at doing the things an automobile was supposed to do, while the 750 Spiders were better at doing the things a sports car was supposed to do. In addition, there are a lot fewer 750's left to go around.

It all depends on how hard-core you are when trying to choose between the two series. There's really nothing *wrong* with the later Spiders—they're really very nice, enjoyable cars. It's just that the 750's so thoroughly captivated the people who owned them that they are more highly regarded now.

It's quite easy to spot the 101 Spiders with their larger taillights and side vent-window frames. The much faster Veloce model was also continued for the Spider, and like the earlier model, there were still no external warnings of the extra performance. With top down, the driver had a sonic treat not available with the Sprint. The stock Veloce exhaust systems were quite free-flow, barely suppressing the distinctive high-pitched ripping sound of the 1300 engine at full throttle. In fact, the Spiders were usually driven much harder than the coupes just for the wonderful sound effects.

MODEL: 101-Series Giulietta Sprint, Sprint Veloce
BODY TYPE: two-door coupe
BODY DESIGNER: Bertone
WHEELBASE 93.7 in.
TRACK, FRONT: 50.9 in.
          REAR: 50.0 in.
WEIGHT: 1991 lbs.
BRAKES, FRONT: Alfin drum
         REAR: Alfin drum
COMPRESSION RATIO: 8.5:1 Sprint; 9.1:1, Sprint Veloce
CARBURETION: single downdraft, Solex, Sprint; dual sidedraft Weber, Sprint Veloce
HORSEPOWER: 80 @ 6300 rpm, Sprint; 90 @ 6500 rpm, Sprint Veloce
AXLE RATIO: 9/41 (4.56) Sprint
                   10/41 (4.10) Sprint Veloce

From the rear, the large taillights completed the identification of a 101 model. The lack of identifying script on the trunk lid was typical of the Giulietta. Jeanette Benson photo.

A perfectly stock-appearing 101-Series Giulietta Spider. Changes from the 750 model included the front side-marker lights, a stretched wheelbase and the nonopening vent windows. The lack of a hood scoop says this isn't a 1600. Jeanette Benson photo.

101-Series Giulietta

ENGINE
Type: In-line four-cylinder
Block: Cast aluminum with slip-fit wet iron liners
Head: Cast aluminum, cross flow, hemispherical chambers
Bore x stroke: 74mm x 75mm
Displacement: 1290 cc (1300 nominal)
Valve actuation: Chain driven, dual overhead cams, bucket
 tappets, shim adjustment
DRIVETRAIN
Transmission: Four-speed, Porsche-type synchromesh, alu-
 minum split-case
Clutch: Single-disc with coil-spring pressure plate, mechanical
 actuation
Driveshaft: Two-piece with front Metalastic joint, double U-
 joint, slip spline and center support bearing
Tire size: 155-15
Wheels: 4 1/2 x 15
SUSPENSION
Front: Double A-arm, sway bar
Rear: Solid axle with longitudinal radius arms and triangular
 lateral locator
Shock absorbers: Tubular, hydraulic

A Giulietta Spider in a very high speed drift. These were very stable
and forgiving cars, very easily driven to their limits. For street driving,
these characteristics allowed emergency maneuvers to be performed
with confidence and a minimum of theatrics. Don Bruno photo.

MODEL: 101-Series Giulietta Spider, Spider Veloce
BODY TYPE: two-place roadster
BODY DESIGNER: Pininfarina
WHEELBASE 88.6 in.
TRACK, FRONT: 50.9 in.
         REAR: 50.0 in.
WEIGHT: 1892 lbs., Spider; 1903 lbs., Spider Veloce
BRAKES, FRONT: Alfin drum
          REAR: Alfin drum
COMPRESSION RATIO: 8.5:1, Spider; 9.1:1 Spider Veloce
CARBURETION: single downdraft Solex, Spider dual sidedraft Webers, Spider Veloce
HORSEPOWER: 80 @ 6300 rpm, Spider 90 @ 6500 rpm, Spider Veloce
AXLE RATIO: 9/41 (4.56), Spider
           10/41 (4.1), Spider Veloce

From 1960 to 1972, this version of the Alfa badge was provided in plastic, and the more expensive and beautiful cloisonne emblem was dropped. Author photo.

The single Solex carburetor and four-into-one cast exhaust header of the Normale engine. The hose that routed under the exhaust header was the capillary line supplying engine oil pressure to the mechanical oil-pressure gauge. The flexible portion tended to harden with age, and if handled roughly would split and thoroughly oil-down the engine compartment. Author photo.

The trunk-mounted battery of the Giulietta and Giulia models was frequently a problem area. Poor starting resulted from corroded connections, particularly the rear chassis ground. And very commonly, leaking battery acid would corrode the battery tray loose from the trunk floor. The next hard, right-hand corner would produce a loud thump and electrical blackout as the battery tipped over and began draining. Periodic maintenance was the cure. Author photo.

CHAPTER 6
SPECIAL-BODIED GIULIETTAS

The nimble, sporting character of the Giulietta chassis and its exceptional sales success ensured that special performance versions would eventually be provided. Both models that resulted—the Sprint Speciale and the Sprint Zagato—exploited excellent aerodynamics and a high state of engine tune to obtain top speed capability in excess of 125 mph from only 1290 cc.

Either of these vehicles offers excellent investment potential plus great enjoyment for the enthusiast. These are very usable, beautiful cars with a huge reservoir of spare parts because they utilize the standard Giulietta engine and chassis components. Body and trim parts are generally not available, but active owner registries exist for both models.

To the collector, these are the most desirable of all the Giulietta models, and are products of a simpler and freer time when such undertakings were still possible. To the enthusiast, they represent the distilled essence of Alfa Romeo—the coming together of exquisite machinery and classic style. They offer beauty that is functional and function that is beautiful.

Sprint Speciale

No one is ever neutral about the appearance of the Sprint Speciale. People will either rave about the beauty of its flowing lines or be completely put off with its unconventional coachwork. To most Alfa owners, this coupe is special indeed, and would be a treasured addition to their collections.

Its controversial styling was derived from the "BAT" aerodynamic exercises conducted by Bertone on the 1900 chassis, and contained a hint or two of the famous Alfa Disco Volante, or "flying saucer," race cars of the early fifties. It certainly is still the most inspired and voluptuous Bertone design that Alfa ever put into production.

The aerodynamics were sufficiently well done to allow the Speciale to reach 124 mph with the 1300 cc Giulietta engine. The Speciale engine was the same Veloce configuration used in the Spider and Sprint, but with the valves shimmed tighter and cams timed for additional overlap to give 116 SAE horsepower.

Giulietta drum brakes were used, but the fronts were given new heavy-duty components with three, instead of two, brake shoes. The rear brakes were the larger assemblies normally used in the front on the other models.

Initially designed with competition in mind, it was simply too heavy and too nice a car for the track. The few victories it did attain were more a tribute to the sturdy Giulietta drivetrain than to the SS chassis.

There were 1,366 Giulietta Sprint Speciales built from 1957 to 1962, when it was upgraded to the Giulia version. Though not as fast as the 1600, the Giulietta Speciale has more of a delicacy and exotic flair about it. Over two decades later it still looks radical and advanced, and the recent trends to aerodynamic design should finally legitimize its styling. Asking prices for Speciales are highly variable. While generally high, they are not yet impossibly priced, and as such are excellent investment candidates. However, if you once acquire one of these lovely cars, you may find it very difficult to ever give it up for mere money.

Sprint Zagato

Alfa Romeo's commitment to ensuring the competition success of its new Giulietta series led once again to Zagato for special lightweight coachwork. Using the floorpan of the short-wheelbase Spider, a delightful aluminum-bodied coupe took shape that would bring an impressive string of victories to both factory and private efforts.

There were two series of the Sprint Zagato, or SZ, produced between 1959 and 1961. The first was known as the "round-tail" for rather obvious reasons.

It had the excellent Giulietta drums at each wheel, although the three-shoe version from the Sprint Speciale (SS) was not used.

Sprint Speciale ★★★★
Sprint Zagato ★★★★★

CHASSIS NUMBERS
1957-1961:   10120.00004-10120.00750——Sprint Speciale
1961-1962:   10120.177001-10120.177624
1959-1961:   10126.00001-10126.00217——Sprint Zagato

The rear of the SS flowed into an abrupt, flat Kamm-tail to reduce aerodynamic drag. Ken Askew has owned this lovely car since new and its excellent aerodynamics may be responsible for his present interest in harnessing the wind. In the background is one of the many windmills Ken has designed and built; efficiency is a contagious approach to life. Author photo.

The emphasis on light weight was unmistakable in every component. Zagato Alfas were particularly satisfying for the manner in which their interiors were relentlessly efficient without leaving a stripped race car impression. Trim items such as headlamp rims and windshield moldings were also of aluminum and likewise astonishingly feather-light. Even the doors, when removed, could be effortlessly lifted with a single finger, and the gauges themselves were the heaviest part of the fiberglass instrument panel.

The SZ shared the 116-SAE-horsepower Veloce engine with the SS. Weighing only slightly over 1,700 pounds, it was by far the fastest of the Giuliettas. To the performance-oriented driver it was also the most desirable, its lightness amplifying all the good Giulietta handling qualities. When *Road & Track* tested an SZ it concluded, "For immediate response in emergencies, this is one of the best cars we have driven."

The SZ felt much more firmly sprung than the production models, especially in roll resistance. It acted like a stable, inert platform that responded almost instantly to the suggestions of its driver. Control efforts were so low that you simply ceased being aware of them. Driving an SZ could easily spoil you for anything else.

It would be perfectly usable on an everyday basis, except for the vulnerability of its completely unprotected coachwork. It was a little short on headroom, but that was the only comfort consideration. The 100-liter fuel tank allowed over 600 miles cruising range.

The second series of SZ featured a completely redesigned body for greater aerodynamic advantage, although it was still based on the steel Giulietta Spider floorpan. Known as the "square-tail" because of its truncated Kamm-effect rear styling, it had a somewhat larger and softer appearance than the round-tail. Its lines are best described as early TZ without the adrenalin.

The front brakes were upgraded to Girling discs, but most of the mechanical specifications were unchanged. Maintenance was no more difficult than with any other Giulietta.

Choosing between these two models of SZ is an agony that any Alfa enthusiast would love to be faced with. They are both highly desirable, with the round-tail having somewhat of an edge. Either version would be an excellent candidate for vintage racing or even running Solo events. Despite the passage of nearly a quarter century, there are still very few 1300 cc cars that can even hope to challenge the performance level of this spirited little coupe.

Asking prices are already moderately high on the Sprint Zagatos and they are rarely offered for sale. As for investment value, one need only contemplate the SZ's uniqueness, competition achievements, historical significance and sporting character to realize it will inevitably come to be recognized as another of Alfa Romeo's classic automotive achievements.

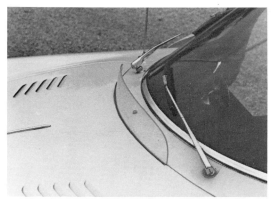

The plexiglass deflector at the base of the windshield was quite functional. Without it, the wipers lifted up at speed and became useless. Author photo.

Those tired of wedge-shaped automobiles could turn to the Sprint Speciale for inspiration. The front grille was very artistically executed and beautifully integrated into the overall styling. Author photo.

MODEL: Giulietta Sprint Speciale
BODY TYPE: 2×2 coupe
BODY DESIGNER: Bertone
WHEELBASE 88.6 in.
TRACK, FRONT: 50.9 in.
        REAR: 50.0 in.
WEIGHT: 2110 lbs.
BRAKES, FRONT: Alfin drum
        REAR: Alfin drum
COMPRESSION RATIO: 9.7:1
CARBURETION: dual sidedraft Webers
HORSEPOWER: 116 @ 6500 rpm
AXLE RATIO: 9/41 (4.56)

The script on the front fenders was one of the few external clues to the Speciale's 1300 engine. Author photo.

The engine compartment layout was standard Giulietta Veloce practice, but the sheetmetal came very close to the carburetors, making their removal difficult. Author photo.

MODEL: Giulietta Sprint Zagato
BODY TYPE: two-place coupe
BODY DESIGNER: Zagato
WHEELBASE 88.6 in.
TRACK. FRONT: 50.9 in.
        REAR: 50.0 in.
WEIGHT: 1890 lbs.
BRAKES. FRONT: Alfin drum
        REAR: Alfin drum
COMPRESSION RATIO: 9.7:1
CARBURETION: dual sidedraft Weber
HORSEPOWER: 116 @ 6500 rpm
AXLE RATIO: 9/41 (4.56)

The SZ engine compartment was very tight-fitting, and the hood barely cleared the oil filler cap. Author photo.

A square-tail SZ. One can easily see the development of aerodynamic ideas and styling that led to the GTZ in 1963. Factory photo.

The SZ interior was racer-Spartan yet very comfortable for touring. The entire instrument panel was a one-piece fiberglass casting and was feather-light. The original floor covering consisted of foam-backed vinyl pads. These were light but also quite fragile, explaining the use of carpeting in this car. Author photo.

British Columbia's "beautiful" license plate on the SZ, and no Alfisti would disagree. The unique oval taillights have been traced to the Italian-built Dauphine that Alfa at one time assembled for Renault. This car has the optional glass side and rear windows. The 15-inch Elektron alloy Campagnolo wheels were very light, strong and desirable. Author photo.

Bill Biggs suspects his beautiful SZ was the one pictured in a very embarrassing upside-down attitude on page 282 of the book *Alfissimo!* by David Owen, based on some unique underbody and exhaust system details. Author photo.

The 2600 Series was introduced in 1962 as an upgrading for the old two-liter cars. The bodies and chassis were obvious carryovers with minor trim changes. The engine was a new design—a big, hefty, high-rpm twin-cam six that showed much Giulietta influence. It represented a deliberate move by Alfa Romeo back toward the larger sports-touring market it had abandoned with its smaller but highly successful four-cylinder models.

Technically interesting and very appealing to the eye, the 2600 never really caught on, and sales figures were disappointing. Only 2,092 Berlinas, 6,999 Sprints and 2,255 Spiders were produced, and production ended in 1968. A few limited series were produced by OSI and Zagato.

Perhaps the 2600 suffered most by comparison to Alfa's own Giulietta and Giulia series. These modern four-cylinder cars were such delights to drive that the more deliberate, slower responses of the six-cylinder machines appeared dated. While seeming somewhat anemic during normal driving, the 2600 came to life and offered surprisingly strong performance at higher speeds.

At the beginning of the muscle car era in the U.S., the subtleties of such an elegant touring machine were simply not appreciated. Yet at approximately $5,000 for the Spider and $7,000 for the coupe, these cars were incredible bargains; I consider it one of my major car-buying oversights not to have purchased one at the time.

Almost all mechanical pieces are still available with diligent scrounging. The transmission is shared with the four-cylinder cars. Body and trim parts are much more difficult to find; acquiring a parts-car is definitely recommended.

The 2600 engine and chassis were very understressed and long-lived. The only real problem area seemed to be in head-gasket longevity. Careful attention to mating surface cleanliness, surfacing the head to ensure flatness, and checking linear protrusion above the block during a head-gasket replacement will help ensure longer gasket life.

The triple Solex 44 PHH carburetors on the Sprint, Spider and Zagato models had somewhat of a bad reputation for both performance and burned valves. These Solexes did not have the usual feature of one throat directly feeding each cylinder. Rather, the manifold was a common-log design with all cylinders communicating into a single chamber which drew from the entire bank of carburetors. In addition, the two throats of each carburetor were actually a primary and secondary, and for low-power requirements only the one primary throat of each carburetor was utilized. A vacuum diaphragm on each carburetor opened the secondary throat butterflies at higher airflow rates.

The complex set of adjustments for these units, some requiring removal of the carburetors, probably accounted for many of the difficulties reported by owners. Weber carburetors were a highly prized factory option that noticeably enhanced performance and were simpler to tune. Many 2600's were converted by owners, but this requires a special intake manifold, which is now in very short supply.

Berlina

The 2600 Berlina was a vehicle that only a determined Alfisti could love. It continued the Alfa tradition of deliberately homely sedans that won over the knowledgeable on the basis of their innards. In a car of this size, cuteness simply didn't work as well as it did on smaller vehicles.

At the same time, the Berlina was far more comfortable and quiet than the coupe or Spider. The rear seating accommodations were certainly superior, as well as the trunk capacity. It was, in fact, exactly what it was intended to be—a secure, comfortable high-speed touring machine for four people and their luggage.

Very few of these sedans were sold in the U.S., and they rarely can be found for sale. As a result, determining a market value would be mere guesswork, and actual prices would depend primarily on the vehicle's condition and the state of mind of both owner and prospective buyer. Judging from pat-

Berlina ★★★
Sprint ★★★
Spider ★★★★
Special-Bodied 2600's ★★★★

CHASSIS NUMBERS
1962-1968: 10600.800001-10600.801511——Berlina
1962-1966: 10602.820001-10602.826403——Sprint
1962-1965: 10601.191001-10601.193155——Spider
1965-1967: 10612.865001-10612.856105——Special Bodied (2600 SZ)

Scott Shadle purchased this 2600 Berlina from the Italian embassy where it was used as a staff car. It was later acquired by Bobcor and eventually dismantled for parts. Scott Shadle photo.

terns established in the other Alfa product lines, the Berlina should probably not sell for more than a comparable Sprint coupe, although the sedan's rarity in America could equalize matters.

A 2600 Berlina would certainly be a conversation piece, even at Alfa gatherings. If the large twin cam engine fails to impress, you can always point out the five-speed column shift.

Sprint

The 2600 Sprint was introduced in 1962 as a replacement and upgrading for the underpowered 2000 Sprint. Visually the two series were identical, with only minor trim and script differences. The six-cylinder engine fit remarkably well into a chassis originally intended for the four-cylinder 2000. A change to four-wheel disc brakes was the only other significant mechanical revision.

Almost seven thousand 2600 Sprints were built until the line was discontinued in 1966. Many more found their way into the U.S. than the earlier 2000 version, leaving the 2600 as the series of choice if one desires a "big" Alfa coupe of this vintage.

When new, the 2600 Sprint was an elegant and expensive vehicle. It was priced at nearly double the smaller Giulia coupe, and even above most domestic luxury cars of the time. The interior was well appointed, and included such unexpected features as power windows, although they were almost laughably slow.

The sporting nature of the car's mechanicals frequently led to incorrect assumptions as to its character. In reality, it was somewhat ponderous to drive at lower speeds with heavy steering and lots of understeer. Once over 100 mph, these qualities were suddenly appreciated for the effortless stability they provided.

The 2600 Sprint is perhaps more desirable today as a collectable Alfa than it was as a new car in the sixties. While exhibiting occasional vintage touches, it is mechanically still quite advanced. The parts situation is a little difficult but not impossible. The 165-400 size tires are becoming scarce as well.

The lack of a performance-car image has held down the price, making it a very good value for its level of sophistication and finish.

Corrosion areas to watch for are the typical ones for Bertone cars of this period—rocker panels, lower front quarter-panel and rear wheelwell arches.

Spider

Only 2,255 of the 2600 Spiders were built between 1962 and 1965. More Spiders were imported to the U.S. than the other model of the series, and as a result they are the most available 2600 today.

Like the Sprint, the 2600 Spider body and chassis were those of the earlier 102-Series 2000 Spider. Although there were only minor changes to the body with the changeover to the 2600 engine from the 2000, they produced a substantial change in the car's character. The 2000 version appeared much lighter and more graceful with its twin hood nostrils and simpler grille. The full-width hood scoop and offset fog lights of the 2600 created a more formidable appearance.

The elegant coachwork by Touring gave a misleading appearance of high performance, particularly with the close resemblance to the Vignale-bodied 3500 Maserati roadsters also being made at the time. Although designated a 2+2, the rear seats were primarily a package shelf. Fit and finish of the body and trim were quite good.

While either the four- or six-cylinder version would be an interesting collector car, the 2600 would be preferred for the improved performance and better availability of parts. The instrument cluster is beautifully executed in the classic tradition with lots of large, round gauges to inform the driver.

Like the other 2600 models, the Spider is primarily a high-speed touring machine despite its sports-car appearance. Handling is just a bit on the vintage side, and it simply does not take to being tossed around Giulietta-style. Ride quality and directional stability are superb.

As the lightest of the production models, the Spider has the easiest steering and somewhat better acceleration. The view from the driver's seat over that long classic hood is very inspiring. The 2600 Spider has been overlooked until fairly recently, and prices are just beginning to increase. As the more sporting model, it commands somewhat of a premium over the Sprint coupe.

Special-Bodied

With the introduction of the six-cylinder engine, coachbuilders turned their attentions to the 2600 chassis, and several interesting vehicles resulted. A four-door 2600 De Luxe by OSI provided a much more attractive sedan than the factory-designed Berlina, although still not as handsome as the Sprint. Only fifty-four De Luxes were built, and if any are in the U.S., they are well hidden.

More available in America, although only 105 were built, is the 2600 Zagato. Surprisingly for Zagato, the body was completely fabricated in steel. Even so, it was approximately 300 pounds lighter

MODEL: 2600 Berlina
BODY TYPE: four-door sedan
BODY DESIGNER: factory
WHEELBASE 107.1 in.
TRACK, FRONT: 55.1 in.
        REAR: 53.9 in.
WEIGHT: 3036 lbs.
BRAKES, FRONT: disc
         REAR: disc
COMPRESSION RATIO: 8.5:1
CARBURETION: dual downdraft Solex
HORSEPOWER: 130 @ 5900 rpm
AXLE RATIO: 8/41 (5.13)

106-Series 2600

ENGINE
Type: In-line six-cylinder
Block: Cast aluminum
Head: Cast aluminum, cross flow, hemispherical chambers
Bore x stroke: 83mm x 79.6mm
Displacement: 2584 cc (2600 nominal)
Valve actuation: Chain driven, dual overhead cams, bucket
    tappets with shim adjustment

DRIVETRAIN
Transmission: Five-speed, Porsche-type synchromesh, alumi-
    num split case
Clutch: Single-disc with coil-spring pressure plate, hydraulic
    actuation
Driveshaft: Two-piece with front Metalastic joint, double U-
    joint, slip-spline and center support bearing
Tire size: 165 x 400
Wheels: 400 mm rim

SUSPENSION
Front: Double A-arm, sway bar, coil springs, kingpins
Rear: Solid axle with longitudinal radius arms and triangular
    lateral locator, coil springs
Shock absorbers: Tubular, hydraulic

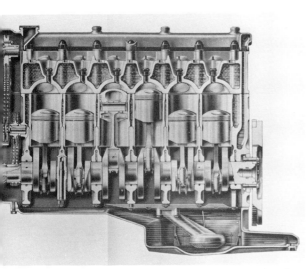

The 2600 engine utilized many of the design features of the Giulietta. The long crankshaft was
rigidly supported in seven main bearings, and twin
overhead camshafts with hemispherical combustion chambers were used. The oil sump was unusual
for its positioning to the rear of the engine, a characteristic of the 1900. Factory artwork.

The notorious triple Solex 44 PHH carburetors of
the 2600 provided very acceptable performance
with proper adjustment and regular lubrication of
the secondary throttle mechanism to ensure free
movement. Author photo.

than the standard 2600 Sprint, giving a noticeable improvement in steering effort and acceleration. The prototype, shown at Turin in 1963, had a one-piece hood and fenders that hinged forward, plus a somewhat contrived tail. That car now lives in the Alfa factory museum. The production version that followed had a conventional engine compartment and hood arrangement plus a much improved and simpler tail design.

The 2600 SZ was certainly unusual, although interesting in appearance. The interior was very nicely appointed, highlighted by a beautiful wood-faced instrument panel. Some of the domestic manufacturers' recent aerodynamic exercises such as the GM Aero-X car bear a striking resemblance in shape, so Zagato's styling may turn out to be prophetic.

As with most special-bodied Alfas, all the mechanicals were standard production parts.

Because of its nonracing orientation, the 2600 SZ has not appreciated to the same extent as the more sporting Alfa Zagatos, although it is the highest priced model of the 2600 series. It is an exceptional value considering its uniqueness, rarity and heritage.

MODEL: 2600 Sprint
BODY TYPE: two-door coupe
BODY DESIGNER: Bertone
WHEELBASE 101.6 in.
TRACK, FRONT: 55.1 in.
REAR: 53.9 in.
WEIGHT: 2816 lbs.
BRAKES, FRONT: disc
REAR: disc
COMPRESSION RATIO: 9.0:1
CARBURETION: triple sidedraft Solex
HORSEPOWER: 145 @ 5900 rpm
AXLE RATIO: 9/43 (4.78)

The 2600 Sprint offered very nice detailing and fit in an elegant package. Tom Tann photo.

The 2600 Spider cockpit was a most inviting place for the enthusiast with its excellent instrumentation and comfortable seating. The rear seating was there in case you really needed it, but legroom was almost nonexistent. Grab handle was for nervous passengers who just didn't understand. Author photo.

The handsome 2600 Spider was one of Alfa's smoothest, most comfortable roadsters. The Touring body was every bit as well-constructed and good-looking as the similar Maserati roadsters of the same period. Borrani wire wheels were available and gave the 2600 a more delicate appearance, but were also a maintenance problem. Author photo.

MODEL: 2600 Spider
BODY TYPE: two-place roadster
BODY DESIGNER: Touring
WHEELBASE 98.4 in.
TRACK. FRONT: 55.1 in.
         REAR: 53.9 in.
WEIGHT: 2684 lbs.
BRAKES. FRONT: disc
         REAR: disc
COMPRESSION RATIO: 9.0:1
CARBURETION: triple sidedraft Solex
HORSEPOWER: 145 @ 5900 rpm
AXLE RATIO: 9/43 (4.78)

Today, the removable hardtop for the 2600 Spider is a rare and highly coveted item. Author photo.

The 2600 Spider's soft top did not have the compact, trim appearance of the Giulietta and Giulia soft tops because of the need to accommodate the four-place seating. Jeanette Benson photo.

Here is the highly prized Weber carburetor setup on a 2600 SZ; most had the same triple Solex arrangement used on the Sprint and Spider. Tom Tann photo.

The rear of the 2600 SZ was not as striking as the front. The C-pillar and rear window contour had a Ferrari Lusso suggestion to them. The taillights were the same as used on the Sprint coupe. Don Bruno photo.

A very elegant wood panel with an excellent instrument cluster arrangement graced the interior of the 2600 Zagato. The large-diameter, thin-rim steering wheel lent a vintage touch. Heating controls were shared with the 105-Series Giulia models. Author vehicle. Author photo.

The 2600 Zagato coupe did not have a conventional styling element in any aspect of its appearance. The large grille and rounded front were somewhat reminiscent of the 6C-2500. Tom Tann photo.

CHAPTER 8
101-SERIES GIULIA

The changeover from the Giulietta to the Giulia Series occurred as a gentle transition. The larger-displacement 1600 cc engine was simply substituted into the existing 101-chassis vehicles beginning with the 1962 model year. Minor trim and interior changes accompanied the new engine.

The most noticeable effect was a smoother, less fussy engine that maintained or improved upon the Giulietta's performance. Gone forever was the torqueless, rev-forever characteristic of the 1300. The stroke increase from 75 mm to 82 mm made for a more serious, powerful feel and the familiar, high-pitched exhaust rasp developed a noticeably lower tone.

Other improvements soon became apparent. Suddenly there was enough heat available to make winter use comfortable. The Spider top became a little more weather-tight. City traffic required much less "rowing," and spark plugs suddenly had much less tendency to foul.

There is no real major difference between the Giulietta and Giulia 101-Series vehicles other than the obvious one of engine displacement. This is generally reflected in their pricing as well as the perception of their desirability, although the Giulia would doubtlessly be easier to live with and maintain.

Far more dramatic changes were soon to follow. With the new engine successfully in production, Alfa's engineers turned their attentions to the chassis and body designs. An entire new range of vehicles resulted—the 105-Series cars. Their success over the following decade solidly established Alfa as a high-volume exotic car manufacturer, and clearly demonstrated the Giulietta phenomenon was not to be a one-time fluke.

Sprint

There was very little to differentiate the 101 Giulia Sprint from the final Giulietta version other than the engine upgrading and five-speed transmission. The external script was changed to show the larger displacement, and subtle interior trim and instrumentation improvements were made throughout the production life of the vehicle.

Although dropped with the introduction of the new 105-Series Sprint GT, the 101 Giulia Sprint was actually put back into production in 1964 with a 1300 cc engine to satisfy customer demand. This revived edition was only available in Europe, and 1,710 of them were produced before production ended again in 1965.

The 101 Giulia Sprint was only available in the single Solex carbureted Normale version; a Veloce model was unfortunately never provided.

If you like the style and lines of the early Bertone Sprints, the Giulia version will provide the least fuss and bother from a parts, maintenance and driveability standpoint. It simply has the advantage of more years of development and debugging behind it, plus the extra flexibility of the Giulia engine.

The pricing of these models is fairly equivalent to the Giulietta coupes, reflecting the essentially unchanged appearance. These are very nice, pleasant cars that are still very affordable. They will most likely slowly and steadily increase in value.

Spider/Spider Veloce

Like the Sprint coupe, there was little substantial change to the design of the Spider with the change to the Giulia engine and five-speed transmission. A hood bulge, which was nicely formed into a full-width scoop, was provided to clear the taller block of the 1600 engine and is the quickest way to identify these models.

Despite a steep 5.12:1 axle ratio, the Normale version was quite economical, and would deliver highway mileage in the mid-thirties.

In 1965, a Veloce version was released with the same 129-SAE-horsepower engine as used in the special-bodied Sprint Speciale and GTZ models. With a 4.10 axle and weighing 2,150 pounds, it was the fastest of the regular production Giulias. Fuel economy suffered from the higher state-of-tune

Sprint
Spider ★★★
Spider Veloce ★★★

CHASSIS NUMBERS		
1962:	10112.350001-10112.350975	Sprint
1962-1964:	10112.352001-10112.359106	
1962:	10123.370001-10123.371096	Spider
1962-1965:	10123.372001-10123.374935	
1964-1965:	10118.390001-10118.391091	Spider Veloce

The 101-Series Giulia Sprint was almost identical in appearance to the 101 Giulietta Sprint. The Giulia script on the front fenders and the side-marker lights were the few identifying marks of this later car. Author photo.

and the loss of the vacuum advance feature with the use of dual Weber carburetors, but *Road & Track* found it to be "an excellent sports car by any standards."

The Giulia Spiders have not paced the rapid appreciation in asking price of the Giulietta Spiders. This is somewhat puzzling in light of higher performance levels and improved reliability the Giulia models offer. Perhaps more than anything, it reflects the special regard Alfa owners have for the uniqueness of the early Giulietta Spiders, particularly the highly tuned Veloce.

The 750 Giulietta Spider's advanced design also had the advantage of a dramatic entry into the marketplace that was not enjoyed by the competent but more familiar Giulia.

In any case, the lower cost preserves a reasonable opportunity to savor these mid-sixties roadsters without a major financial commitment. Eventually nostalgia and increasing scarcity should affect the price of the Giulia Spiders as well, but the increases probably won't be as dramatic.

MODEL: 101-Series Giulia Sprint
BODY TYPE: two-door coupe
BODY DESIGNER: Bertone
WHEELBASE 93.7 in.
TRACK. FRONT: 50.9 in.
          REAR: 50.0 in.
WEIGHT: 1991 lbs.
BRAKES. FRONT: disc
          REAR: Alfin drum
COMPRESSION RATIO: 9:1
CARBURETION: single downdraft Solex
HORSEPOWER: 92 @ 6200 rpm
AXLE RATIO: 8/41 (5.13)

The Sprint interior was comfortable yet sporting. The instrument panel layout changed very little over the production life of the Sprint, although the gauges were updated with the introduction of the Giulia. Author photo.

The later Sprints featured larger taillights but otherwise were difficult to identify. Jeanette Benson photo.

MODEL: 101-Series Giulia Spider, Spider Veloce
BODY TYPE: two-place roadster
BODY DESIGNER: Pininfarina
WHEELBASE 88.6 in.
TRACK, FRONT: 50.9 in.
     REAR: 50.0 in.
WEIGHT: 2130 lbs., Spider; 2150 lbs.. Spider Veloce
BRAKES, FRONT: disc
     REAR: Alfin drum
COMPRESSION RATIO: 9.1:1, Sprint; 9.7:1, Sprint Veloce
CARBURETION: single downdraft Solex, Spider; dual side-
   draft Webers, Spider Veloce
HORSEPOWER: 104 SAE @ 6200 rpm, Spider
             129 SAE @ 6500 rpm, Spider Veloce
AXLE RATIO: 8/41 (5.13), Spider; 9/41 (4.56), Spider Veloce

The interior of the Giulia Spider was little changed from the Giulietta. A glovebox door was added, the instrument markings were refined and a handsome aluminum-spoked steering wheel was provided. The wheel's central hub had two concentric rings—one to blow the horn and the other to flash the lights. The famous "umbrella handle" handbrake still refused to go away. The heavily padded dash panel on this car is not standard. Author photo.

Unlike some roadsters, the Giulietta and Giulia Spiders did not lose their sporty appearance with the soft top in place; if anything, their jaunty look was enhanced. Author photo.

The large taillights help identify this as a Giulia Spider, while the trunk lid lettering tells if it is a Normale or Veloce. However, this can be misleading as cars were frequently converted depending on whether the owner wanted to improve performance or tractability. Author photo.

The Veloce version of the Spider was much faster, and the only giveaway was the six extra letters on the trunk lid. Author photo.

To help clear the slightly taller 1600 engine, the Giulia Spider acquired
a hood scoop and the central chrome strip disappeared. This car has
the very desirable Pininfarina removable steel hardtop. Author photo.

With 101-Series Giulietta and Giulia Spiders side-by-side, the only noticeable difference is the Giulia's hood scoop. Author photo.

CHAPTER 9
105-SERIES GIULIA

The first 105-Series Giulia, the Giulia T.I. sedan, was introduced in 1962 at Monza. The chassis was a completely fresh but evolutionary design that would eventually be used over a wide range of models. The 105-Series Alfas have proven to be the most successful ever in terms of total sales, except for the high-volume Alfasud, and the basic design is still produced in 1983 as the 2000 Spider Veloce.

The most obvious changes were in the front suspension. The double wishbone arrangement of the 101 was replaced with a single lower A-arm and two separate upper links that permitted castor adjustment. Grease fittings all but disappeared, and sealed, maintenance-free pivots were adopted. The tall, narrow, 155-15 tires on 4.5-inch-wide rims were retained from the 101 cars.

A new safety awareness was seen in the new steering linkage that permitted an extremely short steering column with the steering box mounted well behind the wheels. Here was a crashworthy design that anticipated such regulations by almost three years. It worked well enough that it met all subsequent U.S. requirements for steering-column intrusion during crash testing without any obvious modification.

The rear suspension continued as the proven solid axle setup with coil springs and locating linkage. The triangular link of the 101 Series was replaced by a large pivoting T-arm assembly for lateral axle location.

Dunlop disc brakes were incorporated at all four wheels and power brake boosters became available for the first time on the smaller cars. Because of corrosion difficulties and the need for frequent adjustment, the Dunlop brakes were replaced with ATE's, in 1967. Although not a simple conversion, many owners have updated their early 105 Alfas to the ATE brakes. This is a very worthwhile change, and is best accomplished by simply installing the front spindle assemblies and complete rear axle from any 1967 Giulia parts-car. If the brakes are taken from a post-1967 Alfa, the special limiting valve in the rear brake circuit must also be used to maintain the correct front-to-rear proportioning. The Dunlops really can be made to work satisfactorily—it's just that they require frequent periodic attention.

The 101-Series Sprint and Spider continued in production alongside the new sedan while replacements were developed. The new 105-Series coupe appeared first in 1963 as the Giulia Sprint GT, and the new Spider eventually followed in 1966. Both these models boasted dual, side-draft Weber carburetors, although the state of tune was somewhat reduced from previous Webered versions for improved driveability.

The front frame crossmember of the new 105 chassis interfered with the earlier oil pan design, so a new sump was provided, called a "bat-wing" or "hammer-head." It spread sideways at the front of the engine rather than lengthwise as on the older Veloce. A beautiful, finned, cast-aluminum device that worked well and looked good, it was also low and exposed and prone to breakage on rough roads, which accounts for all the 105 Alfas equipped with owner-installed sump guards.

A two-piece, cast exhaust header gave improved durability over the old Veloce tubular headers with little loss in performance. A mechanical fuel pump was driven by an eccentric on the distributor/oil pump drive shaft. Windshield wipers were still single speed and annoyingly rapid. Many owners discovered the slower "parking" speed of the wiper motor could be utilized with minor rewiring and a new wiper switch with an extra position.

Problems tended to be of the nuisance variety. Heater blower motors occasionally trapped water and seized, but they can be cleaned and repaired. Heater valve diaphragms occasionally would burst, parking brake cables would corrode and intermittent electrical problems resulted from an engine compartment fusebox location. The fuel line from the filter to the carburetors was of a hard plastic which tended to crack and leak from the constant flexing; reinforced neoprene fuel line should be used here, and routed in a loose loop. Sometimes a rear suspension bushing or front suspension trailing link ball joint would fail and produce a frightening clatter, but it is easily and inexpensively repaired.

Giulia T.I. ★
Giulia Super ★★
Sprint GT ★★
GTV ★★

CHASSIS NUMBERS
1962-1967: 10514.400001-10514.443228——Giulia TI
1965: 10526.305001-?——Giulia Super
1963-1965: 10502.600001-10502.612999——Sprint GT
1965-1966: 10502.614001-10502.616517
1965-1968: 10536.240001-10536.252501——GTV

The large flat "Kamm-tail" put the aerodynamic principles developed on the Zagato race cars into an efficient production Alfa. There were three different sizes of Giulia sedan taillights. Don Bruno photo.

These are truly delightful, sturdy cars with no major flaws, and are as reliable as exotic sporting vehicles ever get. Many consider them the last of the "real" Alfas because they represent the factory's final design efforts unclouded by the intrusion of government regulation.

The 105-Series Giulias are still reasonably priced, and many good bargains are to be found. While their relatively large numbers and similarity to later models will discourage rapid appreciation, really excellent examples are beginning to command a considerable premium.

T.I./Super

It would have been quite easy, back in 1962, to overlook the significance of the new Giulia T.I. (Turismo Internationale) sedan. But it provided the first glimpse of Alfa's newest chassis, a design that would be the basis of an entirely new range of cars.

Alfa proclaimed the Giulia T.I. to be "The car designed by the wind." Indeed, the rounded front end, flush grille and side glass, body fluting, subtle roof spoiler and the Kamm-effect trunk showed the influence of wind-tunnel testing and the lessons learned developing the SZ and GTZ racers.

Despite its boxy appearance, the drag coefficient of 0.34 was lower than the sportier coupe and roadster models.

The front suspension members of the GTZ were also very similar in configuration to the new 105-Series pieces on the T.I., and it would be very difficult to determine if one were the basis of the other, or if they were simultaneous developments. In any case, it demonstrated again the close interplay between Alfa's competition and production designs.

The T.I. was an extremely smooth and quiet car to drive, and introduced Alfa's first four-wheel power disc brake system on the four-cylinder cars although it originally had the excellent Alfin drum system. It also had a finger-tip-effort five-speed column shift. The front seats would fully recline and the rear seat cushions reversed to provide a fairly level and comfortable surface. Many have used this feature for overnight camping or a quick nap in a rest area.

The factory competition version, called the T.I. Super, started a predictable clamor among enthusiasts for a higher-performance model. The result was the Giulia Super, perhaps the spunkiest four-door Alfa ever sold in the U.S.

For this upgrading, the T.I.'s single Solex carb was replaced with dual Webers. A "proper" floor-mounted shift, more sporting instrument panel, and a taller axle ratio were provided. The result was a car that was light and perky to drive, with almost an adolescent air about it.

Owners tend to be somewhat fanatical, reflected in the fact that it is the only four-door Alfa to have its own registry. If you want an Alfa sedan, this one is the most fun by far.

It is very difficult to find a low mileage Giulia sedan. Many were purchased as everyday cars, and it is not uncommon for odometers to be on the second or third time around. Because of its entertaining character, the sedan asking prices approach those of the coupe.

The 1967 was the last Giulia Super brought into the U.S. market. In Europe it was kept in production right through the seventies in a variety of configurations. Smaller-displacement versions called the Giulia 1300 T.I. and Giulia 1300 Super were very popular. They were both updated with many chassis refinements and a mildly restyled grille in 1974. Appropriately enough, they were then named the Giulia Nuova Super 1300 and 1600, or the New Giulia Super. A diesel-powered Super even appeared in 1976 as a response to the fuel shortages.

Sprint GT/GTV

The long awaited replacement for the Giulietta/Giulia Bertone coupe was finally shown at Frankfurt in 1963. The evolutionary styling was credited to Giugiaro at the Bertone studio. Significantly, the coachbuilder's emblem read "Designo de Bertone," reflecting the fact that the new vehicle was now being built by Alfa at its new factory at Arese just outside Milan. The lines were clearly derived from the 2000/2600 Sprint, also by Giugiaro, while retaining subtle traces of the previous Giulietta model.

The mechanicals were no surprise, since the 105 chassis components were already in production on the Giulia T.I. sedan.

The interior underwent a thorough modernization, with a decidedly sporty flavor, and the old Sprint coupe that everyone liked so much suddenly seemed quite dated. Everything about the new car seemed an improvement.

For 1967, the Sprint GT became the Sprint GTV, or Veloce. Compared to previous applications of the Veloce designation, this new model was in a considerably lower state of tune despite the dual Weber carbs. The claimed three-horsepower gain over the Sprint GT was attributed to tapered and narrowed inlet porting that improved high-speed airflow into the cylinders.

The piston barrels were a precision, tapered slip fit into the block. This "wet-liner" design provided uniform and complete cooling around each cylinder. Thin rubber seals around the bottom flange of the barrels kept the coolant from leaking into the sump. The six small holes were oil passages providing lubrication to each cam journal in the head. Oil returned to the sump by drainback through the front timing chain compartment and the three rear oval slots. The four oblong slots beside each barrel provided coolant to the head. Don Bruno photo.

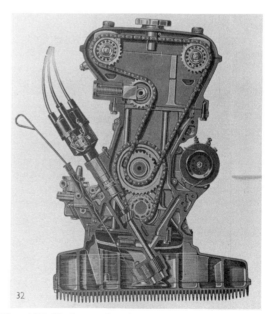

The 105 Giulia engine featured a wide, cast aluminum oil sump. Factory artwork.

This time, Veloce meant primarily a revised trim package. Deeply contoured, very low-seating buckets and a wood-grained instrument panel were the major changes. Externally, the C-pillar acquired a beautiful round green-and-ivory cloisonne emblem of the "quadrifoglio" or four-leaf clover—Alfa's famous racing emblem since the thirties.

The 105-coupes were much closer in character and feel to their roadster counterparts than previous Alfa designs. The GTV, for example, was very close to the Duetto in all performance measurements, and performed equally well in a slalom or track situation. The weather sealing and winter comfort were excellent, although the seals in the vent window area allowed an annoying wind whistle that persisted until production of the coupe ended in 1974.

The flush external door handles were frequently criticized for being awkward to operate. It was really a matter of both maintenance and technique. With the latch properly adjusted and lubricated, the door handle is best operated with a one-handed pinching approach rather than just pulling upward, which seems to have a binding effect. Besides, lifting upward too forcefully can break the handle casting.

These are very nice cars for someone wanting an everyday usable but slightly older Alfa. They have all the modern Alfa attributes and no major flaws. Prices depend heavily on condition, and are close to but somewhat less than those of a comparable Duetto, giving yet another example of the emotional preference for the top-down models. The excellent competition record of these coupes and their lightweight derivative, the GTA, has helped keep their asking prices quite close to those of the roadsters. The primary corrosion areas to be alert for are in the double-box-section rocker panels, the front quarter-panels and the rear wheel arches.

MODEL: Giulia T.I., Super
BODY TYPE: four-door sedan
BODY DESIGNER: Factory
WHEELBASE 98.82 in.
TRACK, FRONT: 51.6 in.
       REAR: 50.0 in.
WEIGHT: 2300 lbs., TI; 2320 lbs., Super
BRAKES, FRONT: disc
        REAR: disc
COMPRESSION RATIO: 9:1
CARBURETION: single downdraft Solex, T.I.; dual sidedraft Webers, Super
HORSEPOWER: 104 SAE @ 6200 rpm, T.I.;
            112 SAE @ 5500 rpm, Super
AXLE RATIO: 8/41 (5.13), T.I.; 9/41 (4.56), Super

The Giulia T.I. instrument panel and steering wheel were not overly inspirational to the enthusiast. This car has been updated from the five-speed column shift to a floor shift, and a console added. Don Bruno photo.

The Giulia Super instrument panel was redone with the more sporting driver in mind. Proper round dials in an antiglare enclosure and the metal-spoke steering wheel were welcome improvements, as was the relocation of the five-speed shift to the floor. A centrally mounted clock was a nice luxury touch, and this was the only Giulia model so equipped. Author photo.

After the introduction of the Super, all Giulia models brought into the U.S. were equipped with the dual Weber carburetors previously reserved just for Veloce models. The cam cover acquired a depression to clear the air intake and allow lower hood lines. Author photo.

The fender fluting, rounded hood and flush grille gave the Giulia sedans excellent air-routing characteristics. Don Bruno photo.

105-Series Giulia

ENGINE
Type: In-line four-cylinder
Block: Cast aluminum with slip-fit wet iron liners
Head: Cast aluminum, cross flow, sodium cooled exhaust valves, hemispherical chambers
Bore x stroke: 78mm x 82mm
Displacement: 1570 cc (1600 nominal)
Valve actuation: Chain driven, dual overhead cams, bucket tappets, shim adjustment

DRIVETRAIN
Transmission: Five-speed, Porsche-type synchromesh, aluminum split-case
Clutch: Single-disc with coil-spring pressure plate, mechanical actuation
Driveshaft: Two-piece with front Metalastic joint, double U-joint, slip spline and center support bearing
Tire size: 155-15
Wheels: 4 1/2 x 15

SUSPENSION
Front: Lower A-arm with upper transverse and longitudinal links, sway bar
Rear: Solid axle with longitudinal radius arms and T-bar locators
Shock absorbers: Tubular, hydraulic

The lattice-work grille of the Sprint GT is the most obvious external difference separating this first 105-Series coupe from the later GTV and GTA. Author photo.

In contrast to the immediate acceptance of the Giulietta Spider, the 1600 Duetto received a somewhat cool initial reception by Alfa enthusiasts. Its styling was a radical departure from the previous 101-Series roadster, although based on Alfa's famous Disco Volante race cars.

Resistance quickly faded after a test drive, and the Duetto soon won acceptance as a very desirable sports car. Pininfarina continued to build this second-generation design for Alfa, and still does in the roadster's present square-tail configuration.

It was first shown at Geneva in 1966, and became available that year as a 1966 model. The Duetto designation was the winner in a name-the-car contest, and reflected the recurring theme of two—two cams, two carbs and two seats for two people to sing a happy song. The Duetto gained unusual notoriety for an Alfa when it starred with Dustin Hoffman in the movie *The Graduate*.

The mechanicals were shared with the 105-Series coupe and sedan. As expected, the lower center of gravity, open cockpit and interesting hoodline contributed to a slightly sportier driving feel than the coupe. The improved ATE brakes and engine porting were acquired in 1967, but no interior upgrading was done as on the other two models. The Duetto did not have the power brake booster.

Weatherproofing was significantly improved over the previous Spider. The heater and defroster outputs were also excellent, making the Duetto Alfa's first frost-free Spider.

The sharply defined edges on the body side-fluting plus the minimal bumper protection made Duettos especially susceptible to parking lot damage. The very low nose tended to underride some large-car bumpers, leading to strange scrapes and dents on the top of the hood. Needless to say, owners soon became quite paranoid about leaving the car unguarded.

Many prefer the aesthetics of this early round-tail or boat-tail configuration over the later square-tail, and it is beginning to show in the price.

MODEL: Duetto
BODY TYPE: two-place roadster
BODY DESIGNER: Pininfarina
WHEELBASE 88.6 in.
TRACK, FRONT: 51.6 in.
REAR: 50.0 in.
WEIGHT: 2195 lbs.
BRAKES, FRONT: disc
REAR: disc
COMPRESSION RATIO: 9:1
CARBURETION: dual sidedraft Webers
HORSEPOWER: 109 @ 6000 (125 SAE)
AXLE RATIO: 9/41 (4.56)

The round-tail Duetto had a very pleasing appearance, but was not as aerodynamically effective as the square-tail Spider that followed it. Jeanette Benson photo.

Duetto ★★

CHASSIS NUMBERS
1966-1967: 10503.660001-10503.666321——Duetto

The Duetto's instrument panel was a modernization of the configuration used in the earlier Spiders. Tom Tann photo.

Ever wonder what happened to Dustin Hoffman's Duetto from *The Graduate*? It now belongs to Dale Macgowan and is still living in the fast lane as an SCCA race car. The sponsor, no doubt, is Robinson Products. Don Bruno photo.

CHAPTER 11
SPECIAL-BODIED GIULIAS

The Giulia engine was used in a delightful variety of special-bodied Alfas. Most of these limited-production vehicles were intended to allow the factory and private customers to compete successfully in a variety of racing categories. They were immensely successful, as even a casual perusal of mid-sixties race results will verify.

Because the competition rules of that era were quite restrictive, the race cars bore a much closer relationship to actual road vehicles than is the case today. This was especially true of the Alfas, and the special series Giulias are extremely desirable collectables as a result.

Drivetrain and chassis parts were shared with the regular production models, so maintenance is a far simpler matter than their low volume would otherwise suggest. The unique body and trim items are the only hard-to-find components; the moral is to make sure the car is complete.

As a rule, they were all street-legal, easily licensed and came with full road equipment, including a decent heating system. Their lighter weight and higher state-of-tune provided considerably enhanced performance gains over the standard models.

To many Alfa enthusiasts, myself included, these vehicles epitomize and define the sports car.

Sprint Speciale

The Sprint Speciale was the only special-bodied Giulia model that had a body design carried over from the Giulietta series. The only external clue to a larger engine was the script on the front quarter-panels that identified the series. Inside the cockpit, there was little change except for a revised instrument cluster. Under the hood, the Giulia engine was given significantly larger tubular headers, and supposedly the front chassis members were slightly widened to accommodate the bulk of the larger pipes. If true, converting a Giulietta may not be as easy as it would first appear.

The brake system was also changed. The three-shoe front drum brakes of the 1300, which were tricky to adjust properly anyway, gave way to Girling discs. The beautiful finned aluminum drums were retained at the rear.

With 129 SAE horsepower from the 1600 cc engine, the Giulia Speciale was significantly faster than its predecessor, and will match or beat the performance of any of the later production four-cylinder Alfas. With its low-drag body, the acceleration at high speed was truly impressive.

From an investment standpoint, there is no reason to prefer a Giulietta Sprint Speciale over a Giulia, or vice-versa. They are both lovely cars and offer an interesting choice between the 1300 and 1600 flavorings. They typically are priced at least double the more common Giulia models, and that gap will no doubt continue to increase. There were 1,400 of the Giulia Sprint Speciales built between 1963 and 1966, making them about equally as available as the Giulietta version with 1,366.

GTZ

The GTZ, or Giulia Tubolare Zagato, is by far the most desirable of all the postwar four-cylinder Alfas. It's the sort of car that reaffirms the enthusiast's faith in legends and completely redefines his concept of lust.

Born to be a racer, the GTZ was actually available in both street and competition trim. Autodelta, Alfa's racing division headed by Carlo Chiti, did the modifications on the cars destined for the track. These consisted of the usual engine changes plus considerably stiffened suspension. The street version shared the same 129-SAE-horsepower-engine setup as the Giulia Sprint Speciale and Spider Veloce. The transmission came with heavy-duty gears and a very quick, short-throw shift lever.

While the engine and transmission were essentially production Giulia, the sump, bell-housing and intake manifold were special castings that compensated for the considerable tilt of the engine. The front suspension was of the general 105-Series configuration, but the links were somewhat longer and did not interchange. At the rear was an elaborate, fully independent setup to minimize unsprung weight.

SS ★★★★
GTZ ★★★★★
GTA ★★★★
GTC ★★★
GSQ ★★★★
T.I. Super ★★★
GTA 1300 Junior ★★★★
Junior Z ★★★
TZ 2 ★★★★★

	CHASSIS NUMBERS	
1963-1965:	10121.380001-10121.381399	SS
1963-1967:	10511.750001-10511.750113	GTZ
1965-1967:	10532.613001-10532.613438	GTA
1964-1966:	10525.755001-10525.755905	GTC
1965-1965:	10123.374639-10123.374935	GSQ
1966-1967:	10508.458608-10508.464286	
1963-1964:	10516.595001-10516.595501	T.I. Super
1968-1972:	10559.775001-10559.775447	GTA 1300 Junior
1970-1972:	10593.1800001-10593.1801110	Junior Z (1300)
1972-1975:	11524.3060001-11524.3060402	Junior Z (1600)
1965-1967:	10511.750114-10511.750125	TZ 2

The Giulia SS had identifying script on the tail and front side-marker lights as the only visible changes from the 1300 model. Inside there was a new instrument panel with all gauges arranged in a straight line. Author photo.

The Tubolare designation referred to the elaborate and exceedingly strong tube frame that provided the structure under the aluminum panels. It had incredible torsional rigidity. If you jacked up under the suspension of one side of it, the wheel on the opposite side would clear the ground almost simultaneously with the first. For a race car, it was a case of massive overdesign. Perhaps that's why these cars never seemed to break up while competing on the rough roads of the Targa Florio, a common fate for many other makes of that era.

The interior fit snugly without being cramped. The emphasis on weight reduction was obvious everywhere, from the fiberglass instrument panel to the very light seats and upholstery. The success could be measured by the GTZ's weigh-in at only 1,450 pounds, making it the lightest Giulia.

On the street, the TZ provided a surprisingly high level of comfort and ride. There was even a heater, although it relied solely on ram-air. The snap-in frames for the side windows seemed the only Spartan touch, but then, they did contribute to the lightness.

Driving a GTZ is a thrill every Alfisti should aspire to. Starting the engine produces a burst of sounds both familiar and new. The rigidly mounted, high-compression engine and the absence of soundproofing bring all the normally muted sounds right up close for your enjoyment. The vibrations drive the aluminum body panels into that unique hollow resonance so characteristic of Zagato Alfas.

Letting out the clutch, the benefits of light weight become immediately obvious, as the TZ springs away with muscle car acceleration, and the short-throw lever gives lightning-quick shifts. Now all the driveline noises can be heard—the thrashings of the transmission and differential gears and bearings, and the whirrings of the half-shaft U-joints. The shriek of the engine on hard acceleration is simply unforgettable, particularly with the "Sebring exhaust" side pipe. And it's all tied together in such a taut, controlled, precise manner, that the driver is drawn into an alertness matching the immediacy of the machine.

At speed, snap off the ignition and flick into neutral. The instant silence shows the superb aerodynamics of the Zagato's shape—there is absolutely no wind noise or buffeting even with the side windows removed. All that can be heard is the tires slapping over expansion joints and the hushed sound of the half-shafts. Suddenly you realize it isn't slowing down—it seems minutes before the speedometer shows a drop in speed.

For serious deceleration, the TZ has four immense Girling disc brakes, the same type used on the racing Jaguars. The rears are mounted inboard on the differential to further reduce the unsprung weight.

No one ever emerges unsmiling from a drive in a GTZ. Grown men have been known to jump up and down with glee while describing their first adventure behind the wheel of one. A more subtle source of enjoyment is the car's excellent pedigree, with a long history of lovely Alfa-Zagato designs extending back into the thirties. Some people don't think such things really matter, but then neither do they understand why a Rembrandt costs so much when the local discount store sells excellent reproductions at bargain prices.

I was fortunate enough to co-own one of these wonderful cars with Tom Tann for eight years. It forever changed the way I evaluate automobiles. To me, the GTZ is *the* definition of a sports car. I doubt I'll ever own anything else I'll enjoy as much. Unfortunately, the rest of the world has caught on, and after a long period of being terribly underpriced, a good GTZ now sells for almost the same as a decent house.

Of the 112 that were built in 1963 through 1967, about a third have been lost through various forms of attrition, primarily the hazards of racing. There are slightly more than a dozen in the U.S., although this number keeps changing as they are imported and exported. They are doing very well in vintage racing, and that's the best place to see them in action today.

GTA

The GTA was the factory competition version of the 105-Series Giulia Sprint GT. Like the GTZ, it was also produced in street and competition versions, with Autodelta again doing the race modifications. Five hundred GTA's were produced between 1965 and 1967, fifty of which were right-hand-drive.

Although appearing virtually identical to the production Sprint GT, all the outer panels were in aluminum, and the side windows were plexiglass. All the interior components—seats, instrument panel and upholstery—were lightened as well, and the resulting car weighed only 1,640 pounds, 450 pounds less than the steel-bodied version.

Knock-off Campagnolo alloy wheels were a racing option to speed up tire changes during a pit stop. Front air scoops are not original but an Autodelta modification to provide adequate cooling for racing. It must have been painful to cut the beautiful aluminum skin. Author photo.

Stunning from any angle, the GTZ will always draw a crowd. Even after complete restoration, as here, a TZ is often judged lower in a concours than an equally well-prepared production model such as an SS. The rougher metal edges and detailing of the Zagato that reflect its racer origins seem to bias the eye of the judges. Author photo.

Under the hood was a twin-plug 1600 cc engine conservatively rated at 133 SAE horsepower. Dual 45 DCOE Weber carbs and tubing headers were standard. While the exhaust was essentially the same configuration as the production car, tubing diameters were somewhat larger. A brake booster and limited-slip differential were highly desirable options. The chassis was standard 105-Series Giulia, with subtle suspension geometry changes to improve handling. The 6x14-inch Campagnolo magnesium wheels were standard.

The GTA was immensely successful in all the categories it was raced. It won the championship in the European Manufacturers' Challenge three years in a row—1966, 1967 and 1968—and dominated the Trans-Am B-Sedan class for years, occasionally winning overall. Its excellent record reflects the inherently robust, burstproof and sporting nature of all the 105-Series Giulias.

On all but the fastest of tracks, the GTA should be able to best a GTZ because of its superior handling.

Driven on the street, the GTA is just about as reliable and practical as its slower look-alike, except it's a lot more fun. The cornering power and acceleration are significantly better, and the ride is very firm, just bordering on harshness.

I've always felt the GTA should have been designated the Veloce version instead of the essentially cosmetic GTV that appeared in 1967. While the GTV is a very nice car, it simply doesn't have the additional fire Alfa's previous Veloce versions led everyone to expect. The GTA's disadvantages are the fragility of the aluminum bodywork in real-world parking lots, the crazing of the plexiglass windows, and the scarce, $150 distributor cap. They should also be kept away from exposure to salt and moisture, or galvanic action will simply detach the aluminum skin wherever it contacts steel framing.

These are tremendously enjoyable cars for the enthusiast. Prices are approximately triple to quadruple the steel-bodied Giulia coupes, but they are still quite reasonable for the performance level and uniqueness they provide. And they don't attract any more attention, legal or otherwise, than any of the other 105-Series coupes, a real problem with the more spectacular-looking special-bodied Alfas.

GTC

In a rather unusual move, Alfa announced a convertible version of its new 105-Series coupe in 1965 at Geneva. This blurred the usual distinction between coupe and roadster models, although it did provide a four-place open car. One thousand of these vehicles, designated the GTC, were built over the next two years.

There are not many GTC's in the U.S., and they are very infrequently seen. They usually bring somewhat of a premium in price over the standard Sprint GT or GTV because of their novelty and scarcity; and because the top goes down.

Since the roof structure was an integral part of the coupe's rigidity, extra bracing had to be added to minimize chassis flexing.

There are two unique problems to watch for when considering a GTC. The first is the condition of the top material, as replacements will be difficult to find. The other is an interior corrosion problem caused by water leaking in around the edges of the soft top. Many of the GTC's have been completely ruined by rusting from the inside out, and the condition isn't very obvious until it's too late.

Otherwise, they have all the Giulia virtues and make interesting collector cars as long as you keep them reasonably dry.

Gran Sport Quattroruote

The Gran Sport Quattroruote, sometimes known as the GSQ, the 4R Zagato or simply the Replicar, was a unique automotive phenomenon. Superficially, it was to be a reproduction of the famous and highly desirable 6C-1750 Zagato-bodied Alfa from the thirties. Commissioned by *Quattroruote*, an Italian enthusiast magazine, Zagato Carrozeria recreated the lines of its original masterpiece around modern Alfa components. Ninety-two of these cars were built from 1965 to 1968. The 101-Series Giulia suspension and drivetrain components were used, with the single-Solex-carbureted Giulia engine squeezed under the narrow hood. The cars were completely assembled and finished by Zagato.

At first, the purists were highly offended and had a wonderful time pointing out all the errors of proportion and detail, particularly the undersized fifteen-inch wheels and the wrong displacement and configuration engine.

Once in the hands of owners, an interesting thing began to happen: People liked them. The detailing was excellent, the workmanship beyond reproach, and they drove and felt like real cars. In fact, being fairly light at only 1,650 pounds, they would out-accelerate most of the other production Giulias.

The Zagato's instrument panel was very lightweight fiberglass, and large, round, very responsive gauges were used. Note the prominence of the 10,000 rpm tachometer in front of the driver and the speedometer positioned to impress the passenger. The Alfetta GT later copied this configuration in the hopes of some competition association, but everyone seemed to miss the point and soundly criticized the layout. Author photo.

Here is the world's first, and possibly last, winter evaluation of the GTZ: Although the car's cammy engine tends to provoke wheelspin, the quick responses and good weight balance provide surprisingly acceptable performance under low-traction conditions. Former author car. Author photo.

The truncated Kamm-tail of the GTZ was used primarily to reduce air drag, but also served well as a billboard. Tom Tann photo.

The Replicar finally has come to be accepted for what it really is—a modern, complete automobile in its own right, with styling to commemorate its famous namesake. For those who really admire the vintage Zagato lines, but don't care for either vintage prices or maintenance, the Replicar is a fascinating and practical alternative. It is comfortable and jaunty, with all the sporting sounds, feel and character one expects of an Alfa.

It has slowly begun to dawn on many people just what a gem the Replicar really is, and they are regretting their missed opportunities to buy one. This has had the expected upward effect on prices, although they still vary widely.

Most Replicars are usually found in good to excellent condition. They are so obviously a specialty car that owners tend to pamper them and keep them sheltered from bad weather.

T.I. Super

It's a little difficult to keep the nomenclature straight on the different varieties of Giulia sedans, but the effort is worthwhile. Otherwise, it would be fairly easy to pass up a T.I. Super, thinking it was just another 1600 four-door.

While not strictly a special-bodied vehicle, the T.I. Super is significant and different enough to warrant consideration in this section.

It was introduced in 1963 as the competition version of the new Giulia sedan, and appeared in both racing and rally applications. Slightly thinner sheetmetal was apparently used, all sound-deadening was left out and nonoperating plexiglass windows were put in the rear doors for a 200-pound weight saving. A floor-mounted five-speed transmission, Campagnolo alloy wheels, lightweight fixed-back bucket seats and a more sporting instrument panel were supplied. It was given the same high-performance engine as used in the Giulia SS and TZ, quite a change from the mild, single Solex version in the Giulia T.I.

Externally there was little to give the car away except the T.I. Super lettering, the large quadrifoglio on the front fenders and the wire mesh covers over the foglight openings which now served as cold air inlets. The T.I. Super was only built for two years, with 501 being made by 1964.

Proponents of the car like to claim that the T.I. Super was used as a development mule for the GTA. The fact that the T.I. Super and the GTA were the only Alfa models homologated in Fédération Internationale de l'Automobile (FIA) Group II lends a good deal of credibility to that viewpoint.

The T.I. Super combined the size, utility and homeliness of the Giulia sedans with the sounds and capabilities of the more sporting models. An excellent "Q-ship," it had performance well in excess of what its appearance would ever suggest.

There are only a handful of T.I. Supers in the U.S., which is unfortunate since they are so entertaining. Since they predate the U.S. safety and emission standards, they would be very easy to import.

T.I. Supers are somewhat of an unrecognized special-interest Alfa, and this has served to keep their price lower than normally expected for a performance model. But this could easily change, making them a good speculation car and potentially a good investment. They are certainly the most fun sedan Alfa's ever turned loose.

GTA 1300 Junior

In 1968 a smaller-displacement version of the GTA was announced. It was aimed primarily at the 1300 cc class of the European Touring Car Championship, which was previously dominated by the Mini-Coopers. Needless to say, the GTA Juniors simply devastated the Minis despite their high state of competition development, and won the championship title many years in a row.

The unique GTA Junior engine utilized the 1600 Giulia bore of 78 mm with a short 67.5 mm throw crankshaft. The GTA twin plug head was added for high-rpm breathing, and all heavy-duty internals were provided. With a stroke ten percent shorter than even the Giulietta and Giulia 1300's, rpm in excess of 9000 was possible. In competition tune it produced 160 DIN horsepower with Webers.

For those who believe the Spica mechanical fuel injection was purely an emissions device, it should be pointed out that a hundred of the competition GTA Juniors were equipped with this system for a five-horsepower gain over the carburetor setup. In all, 300 GTA Juniors were built between 1968 and 1972.

The interior had the same instrument panel configuration as the GTA, but updated to the wood-grain effect as used on the Giulia GTV. The seats and upholstery of the street version, while still noticeably lighter than those of the steel-bodied coupes, were also less Spartan than the very light and fragile GTA equipment.

This GTA is the former Winkler/VanderVate Trans-Am racer that was the Northeast divisional champion in 1965. It was somewhat detuned and returned to street usage. Former author vehicle. Author photos.

In fact, when comparing the street versions of GTA and GTA Junior, the Junior came across as a more solid and quiet car, a result of both additional soundproofing and further chassis development. The weight penalty for all this improvement was only thirty-three pounds.

Like the GTA, the GTA Junior provided incredible cornering ability that is still eye-opening today even for experienced Alfa drivers. The brakes always seemed to simply stop the car from any speed without the slightest fuss, well before the driver had a chance to be amazed at their effectiveness.

The one major difference came from the combination of a close-ratio gearbox and the torque-less 1300 engine. While the GTA could be launched like a dragster, there was really no fast way off the line with the Junior. Drop in the clutch at high rpm and it simply bogged. A gentler start left you accelerating slowly, waiting for the power band to arrive. But once under way the tall first gear and high rpm capability of the engine were a potent combination, saving much shifting in tight corners.

Only a handful of street GTA Juniors was imported to the U.S. The competition versions are more available here, and have been fairly successful in C-Sedan racing. In fact, many GTA's were converted to Juniors with a simple engine substitution, just to race them in a class where they were more competitive.

Because they are so similar, the pricing of a GTA Junior should be much like the GTA's—that is, expensive but not impossibly high. They are great fun to drive, with very high limits of adhesion. Lacking the hot-rod abilities of the 1600 GTA, they offer performance more in the Giulietta Veloce vein, but with a lot more reliability. At Alfa, racing doesn't just improve the breed; with cars like the GTA and GTA Junior, it *is* the breed.

Junior Z

The Junior Z was the last Alfa Romeo produced in collaboration with Zagato. First shown in Turin in 1969, it became available in 1970 with the 1300 Giulia engine, and 1,108 with this displacement were built. In 1972 the Junior Z was upgraded to the torquier 1600 Giulia engine, and 402 of this somewhat faster version were built before production ended in 1975.

At 2,100 pounds, the Junior Z was not as light as normally expected of Zagato designs, although it did have a several-hundred-pound advantage over the other production Alfas of the time. This was primarily due to its steel rather than aluminum body panels. An atypical feature on postwar Alfa-Zagatos, it was only used once before, on the 2600 SZ.

The Junior Z had good aerodynamic features, especially the Kamm-tail and the full-width plexiglass cover that smoothed and flushed the front grille opening. But overall it wasn't nearly as effective or radical as the earlier SZ and GTZ cars, a consequence of being intended primarily for the street rather than competition.

The real attraction of the Junior Z was its small size, which gave it a very nimble, quick feel. Owners praised its handling qualities, frequently describing them in terms of go-cart response, a result of the Z's firm springing and roll resistance. The chassis was based on the familiar and effective 105-Series components.

The interior of the Junior Z was very straightforward and simple, with most components taken from other Alfa production vehicles. There was a surprising amount of room and comfort for the driver. The overall effect was that of a pleasant, no-frills sport coupe. The nonenthusiast, unaware of its potential, might even have described it as "cute," to the great annoyance of its owner.

One unusual feature was the power latching of the rear hatch lid. When the lid was closed, a motor turned a screw mechanism which engaged the lid, fully seating and sealing it. The driver could also reverse the process with an unlock switch, and it was often used on the highway to raise the rear lid slightly and provide flow-through ventilation.

The Junior Z was never imported to the U.S., certification simply being too impractical for such a limited-production vehicle. Besides, the extra weight invariably added by meeting the U.S. standards would have spoiled the car's character and lessened its appeal.

Nevertheless, a good number of Junior Z's have been privately imported and they are more available in the U.S. than would normally be expected. While the 1600 version is certain to be preferred for its extra performance, there seems to be no real price difference between it and the 1300 Z. Asking prices are scattered, but typically are at a good premium over the contemporary production Alfas. The general tendency is upward, making the Junior Z a reasonably good investment as well as a delightful sporting Alfa to own and admire.

TZ 2

In an attempt to offset the power advantage of the Porsche 904, the last twelve cars built on the TZ chassis were a higher-performance version known as the TZ 2. The car was dramatically restyled with

The GTC was the only four-place convertible by Alfa in the entire range of Giulietta-based four-cylinder engines. Jeanette Benson photo.

a much lower, more rakish look. In a bold move for Zagato, the new body was constructed in fiberglass rather than aluminum.

Wider, GTA racing-style wheels were supplied, along with the GTA twin-plug engine for improved high rpm output. The interior became just a bit tighter than the earlier GTZ, which in retrospect was then referred to as the TZ 1.

Currently, there is only one known TZ 2 in the U.S. Having all the good attributes of the GTZ with improved performance and more serious appearance as well, the TZ 2 is a highly desirable and attractive automobile. The fiberglass body has both good and bad features. While far more resistant to denting and corroding than aluminum, it is subject to deterioration of the resins which produce the familiar crazing and separation problems common to fiberglass cars.

A TZ 2 would be expected to be the highest-priced version of the TZ series. Recent transactions in Europe have in fact established a value approximately double the TZ 1, placing it beyond the reach of most enthusiasts.

What could be more fun than a Replicar with top down in an ice-run? Don Bruno photo.

The Replicar looked "real" enough to make people stop for a second and third look. Just a nice Sunday drive on a winding country road. Don Bruno photo.

The taillights were the smallest used in the Giulia sedan series. This wide exhaust-pipe cutout was not typical Giulia practice, but is flared and appears to be original. Don Bruno photo.

The T.I. Super's instrument panel was a definite improvement over the Giulia T.I.'s, and led to an even better configuration on the Giulia Super. Don Bruno photo.

Lightweight, nonreclining seats were used in the T.I. Super, and 6x15 Campagnolo alloy wheels were available. Don Bruno, the owner of this interesting car, is the keeper of the Giulia Sedan registry. Don Bruno photo.

The formidable 110-SAE-horsepower 1300 twin-plug engine of the GTA Junior (with large air hose removed) featured tubular headers and an oil radiator as standard equipment. The dual ignition allowed the use of significantly larger valves by moving the single spark plug out of the top center of the hemispherical combustion chamber. Two spark plugs were then needed to approximate the ignition of the single central plug and thus retain the excellent flame-front characteristics. Author photo.

John Hoard's beautiful GTA Junior has over 100,000 miles yet is still very successful in concours and time trials. All the striping, script and emblems are factory original for this model. Author photo.

The interior of the GTA Junior had more durable upholstery and less radical seating than the GTA. The wood-grained instrument panel was shared with the Giulia GTV. Author photo.

A GTA Junior devoid of its bumpers and side stripes, but with rear wheelwell flares added to compensate. Jeanette Benson photo.

The famed Sebring exhaust was little more than a side-exit, large-diameter straight pipe that bolted directly to the header flanges. A small bulge in the pipe was a feeble gesture to satisfy the requirement for a muffler, and the oval extractor produced truly impressive sounds and power from the 1600 engine. Tom Tann photo.

The TZ 2 was very low-slung and menacing; its appearance left no doubt as to its purpose or potential. Completely at home on the track, the TZ 2 was the last of the streetable racers from Alfa. Tom Tann photo.

The rear hatch of the Junior Z could be left partially open for ventilation. The taillights appeared to be taken from the 1750 Berlina. Tom Tann photo.

The wide BWA wheels and angled, dual-outlet exhaust pipe give a very purposeful look to Paul Heill's beautiful 1300 Junior Z. Author photo.

Nineteen sixty-eight was the first year for U.S. emission requirements. Rather than compromise performance characteristics, Alfa did not offer any '68 vehicles for sale in this country. For 1969, the Spica fuel-injection system was readied, which preserved both power output and driveability. Engine displacement was increased to 1779 cc, close enough to claim kinship to the famous six-cylinder "1750" Alfas of the thirties. This was accomplished by a significant lengthening of the stroke to 88.5 mm from the 82 mm of the 1600. A very flat torque curve resulted that gave the 1750 vehicles a completely different, more serious character than the free-revving Giulias.

The 1750's were only sold for two years in the U.S.—1969 and 1971; there were few, if any, 1970 federalized Alfas. There were significant changes in the '71 version, including a switch from floor-mounted to suspended pedals, the injection pump upgraded to a configuration which lasted through the '81 model year, and offset wrist pins on the pistons which emphasized even more the strong torquey impression.

At the time, an automotive trade pact with Canada provided a loophole that allowed legal importation of Weber-carbureted 1750's. A good number entered the U.S. in this manner, and can often be found titled for the "missing" years of 1968 and 1970.

Berlina

A brand new four-door sedan, the 1750 Berlina, was produced from 1967 to 1972. It was introduced as a 1969 model in the U.S., featuring the new Spica fuel injection. This cut the effective U.S. market sales-life of the Giulia Super quite short by Alfa standards, although it remained in production for the European market up to 1972. The 1750 Berlina was considered an upgrading in both markets. The wheelbase was longer, the body slightly larger in all dimensions and the interior more spacious and plush.

This was accomplished with only a 160-pound weight gain, so the larger engine was able to actually deliver a performance increase. The fuel injection gave additional smoothness and refinement over the carbureted version. When *Road & Track* staff members tested a 1750 Berlina, they were quite impressed with its potential and felt that "The fairly good driver will be able to shock a lot of guys in Corvettes and supercars, not to mention the more traditional live-axle sports cars."

On paper, by all the usual automotive criteria, the new Berlina was a significant improvement over its predecessor. The only loss was the spunky character of the Giulia Super that so endeared it to its owners. Many people, myself included, purchased a 1750 Berlina on the strengths of the Giulia Super only to find out that the lively personality was gone.

Yet the 1750 Berlina was, and remains, an incredibly good value. It is a comfortable, competent, sports-sedan that suffers only by comparison to the more youthful, previous version of itself. Despite its exotic features and creature comforts, the Berlina was, and is, a difficult car to sell and is priced considerably below the other 1750 models. They are perhaps too sporting for the general public and not sporting enough for the typical Alfa customer. Buy a Berlina if you need and appreciate its space, utility value and mechanicals; but don't consider it an investment.

GTV

The 1750 GTV was produced for the European market from 1967 to 1972 in carbureted form using the familiar dual 40 DCOE Weber setup. This model was sold in the U.S. in 1969 and 1971, and significant differences were incorporated between those two model years. There were, of course, the mechanical improvements shared by all the 1750 models, but the coupe underwent some unique upgrading of its own.

The 1969 GTV primarily reflected the changes necessary to meet the new U.S. emission and safety standards with some trim and interior updates to distinguish it from the Giulia coupe. The Spica fuel injection and dual-circuit brakes with two boosters were the most obvious new mechanical features.

CHASSIS NUMBERS		
1967-1972:	10548.1300101-10548.1785485	Berlina
1968-1972:	10571.1555001-10571.1556759	Berlina (U.S.)
1967-1972:	10544.1350001-10544.1376232	GTV
1968-1972:	10551.1533201-10551.1535675	GTV (U.S.)
1967-1971:	10557.1410001-10557.1413036	Spider
1968-1972:	10562.1480001-10562.1484050	Spider (U.S.)

The 1750 Berlina was larger, heavier, faster, and had considerably improved fuel economy over its predecessor, the Giulia Super. The longer 88.6-inch wheelbase with larger wheel excursions gave a much better ride than the coupe and Spider versions. Former author vehicle. Don Bruno photo.

The front-end styling was refined and smoothed, with the hood's leading edge flushed-in and a set of fog lamps added.

The interior was given a completely redesigned instrument panel with a console. The revised seats were given the federally-required head restraints, and featured wild-looking "flying-buttress" side bolsters.

The 1971 1750 GTV was changed extensively from the 1969 model, and is much closer in feel and character to the later 2000 model. The seats were again restyled, becoming a bit more conservative but acquiring an ingenious new feature that has been incorporated in all subsequent Alfa coupes. When the seatback was folded forward to allow access to the back seat, the seat base moved forward as well to facilitate entry, and then returned to its original position as the seatback was pulled back and latched.

The rear taillights were enlarged, an improved configuration that was to last through the end of the coupe's production. Defroster wires were added to the rear window, and they were greatly appreciated by owners in cold or humid climates.

The 1969 and 1971 GTV's shared the same instrument panel and front-end styling. These two years are considered to have the best appearance of all the 105-Series coupe variations. It was a more serious and mature design than the earlier Giulia, and not as busy looking as the 2000 that followed.

There is no real asking price difference between these two model years, yet they offer different features and characters. The 1969 GTV seems the sportier, possibly a result of the lower and more supportive seating, while the 1971 GTV is a bit more refined and improved mechanically. They are both excellent sport coupes with the same performance capabilities as the Spider and offer a lot more comfort and weather protection.

Spider Veloce

Like the GTV, the 1750 Spider Veloce was available in Europe from 1967 through 1971, while it was sold in the U.S. in 1969 and 1971 only.

The 1969 model was virtually identical to the 1600 Duetto in appearance. Only the larger injected engine, rear sway bar, fourteen-inch wheels and the Iniezione script on the trunk lid distinguished it from the earlier car.

Along with the updated engine and suspended pedals, the 1971 Spider was given considerably revised sheetmetal. Wind-tunnel testing had shown that the round-tail design produced high aerodynamic drag, so a new square-tail configuration was readied that significantly reduced wind resistance.

A significant number of other minor body changes were incorporated at this time that served to modernize the Spider's lines without changing its basic appearance. The windshield was made a bit more rakish, the grille was widened and lowered, the door handles flushed-in and the bumpers restyled. There were some structural changes in the floorpan stampings as well, resulting in the square-tail Spiders having a bit less legroom than the round-tail versions. Long-legged drivers will find the 1969 and earlier Spiders a lot more comfortable for this reason.

A completely revised instrument panel with gauges set in two large, deeply shrouded "pods" came with the new square-tail, and is still used in the present production Spider. The convertible top was also restyled and its fit and sealing were considerably improved.

Despite the 1971 Spider being a noticeably improved car, asking prices tend to be higher on the 1969 model. No doubt the limited number of the round-tails and the visual similarity of the '71 model to all the later 2000 Spiders have much to do with this. Either one would be an excellent choice. Both are reliable and entertaining and will provide all the wind-in-the-hair joys for which Italian sports cars are noted.

Spica Fuel Injection

The Spica fuel injection system was a special development for the U.S. emission requirements, and is a significant enough component of the modern Alfa to warrant a closer look. It was supplied on all U.S.-specification Alfas from 1969 through 1981, so it will be featured on the majority of used Alfas you encounter here. The injection pump itself was already being produced by Alfa's Spica division for diesel engine applications, and was modified for gasoline use on the 1750 and eventually the 2000 engine. It was also used in various forms for the Montreal, the GTA Junior race cars, and a version was even put on Alfa's turbocharged, boxer-twelve Formula One engine.

The pump was bolted to the engine front cover, and was pressure-lubricated by the engine's oil system. A fiberglass cog belt drove the pump off the engine front pulley. This operated the pump's front pumping section, consisting of a crankshaft and plungers, plus it provided an rpm and timing reference.

MODEL: 1750 Berlina
BODY TYPE: four-door sedan
BODY DESIGNER: factory
WHEELBASE 101.2 in.
TRACK, FRONT: 52.1 in.
      REAR: 50.2 in.
WEIGHT: 2332 lbs., Europe; 2484 lbs., U.S.
BRAKES, FRONT: disc
      REAR: disc
COMPRESSION RATIO: 9:1
CARBURETION: dual sidedraft Webers, Europe; Spica mechanical injection, U.S.
HORSEPOWER: 118 @ 5500 (135 SAE), Europe; 132 SAE @ 5500, U.S.
AXLE RATIO: 9/41 (4.56)

The instruments of the Berlina were nicely executed and mounted in their own individual molded pods on the panel. Antiglare spokes appeared for the first time on the steering wheel. Don Bruno photo.

The Berlina's overhung trunk lid was a nice styling effect, but tended to trap moisture in the lip and then rust. Undercoating the inside of the rear lip is highly recommended. The large effective area of the tail continued the Kamm-effect aerodynamics of the Super. "Inezione" proclaimed this car to be injected. Don Bruno photo.

The rear section of the pump was a mechanical logic unit which combined various engine and ambient parameters and converted the result into fuel requirement information. This fuel need was expressed by the fore-aft positioning of a single link. This link rotated collars around the plungers by means of a gear rack and this determined the amount of fuel delivered during each stroke. The logic section was capable of responding to throttle position, altitude and the rpm and temperature of the engine.

The plungers were supplied with gasoline by a continuous, high-flow-rate circulation system. The fuel pump was also by Spica, and consisted of an electric motor with an external gear pump. It unfortunately proved to be unreliable because of motor brushes wearing out and the resulting accumulation of carbon powder. Expected life was anywhere between 2,000 and 80,000 miles.

The factory acknowledged this problem in 1975 with a change to a Bosch fuel pump. This was a sealed unit containing both the electric motor and a roller-type pump. The gasoline thus flowed through the motor, cooling it and flushing the carbon powder downstream to the filter, eliminating the build-up problem of the previous unit. Retrofitting a Bosch fuel pump to a pre-1975 Alfa requires reducing the restriction orifice in the injection pump outlet nozzle (the farthest forward of the two fuel-line fittings on the pump) to 1.0 mm. If this is not done, cavitation problems can occur because of insufficient back-pressure, and the engine will starve for fuel.

You should know that there is a division of opinion among owners over the desirability of Spica fuel injection; some love it, others distrust it to the point of replacing it with a dual Weber carburetor setup. My personal feeling is that the Spica injection is one of the most exotic features on the car, and is the nicest thing to come along since twin-cams and aluminum engines. Replacing it with carburetors is like going back to wooden-spoked wheels, and should reduce the value of the vehicle.

What accounts for the disagreement? A variety of factors, any of which can result in poor operation and an unhappy owner. The most prevalent is incorrect adjustment, which can produce poor mileage, sluggish response and hard starting.

Despite Alfa's clear instructions in its injection manual, even professional mechanics often seem to prefer the "twiddling" approach instead of a systematic setting of clearances and linkages. Since all the adjustments interact through the geometry of the mechanical logic in the pump, one improper setting affects the rest. The result is a system in which all the settings eventually become misadjusted, each to compensate for the error in the others. Doing this "by ear" is time-consuming and frustrating, and never will result in optimum performance. Also very important is the injection pump oil filter replacement, every other oil change. Simply following the recommended procedure is the only "secret" to injected happiness.

Once properly adjusted, a Spica-equipped Alfa will match or exceed its carbureted equivalent in the same state-of-tune in all performance aspects. However, it is easy to confuse the Webered engine's eagerness to rev with increased power and responsiveness. It really comes from the carb's accelerator pumps, which squirt a hefty stream of gasoline every time you depress the throttle, but do not give additional power for accelerating. In fact, they waste fuel and carbon the combustion chambers.

Admittedly, fuel injection does have a high intimidation level, and some people convert to carburetors purely because they have a more familiar technology. Yet, owners who have taken the time to learn tuning and repair of the Spica unit, almost universally are surprised by its simplicity and their ability to deal with it. Most express regret at holding back for so long out of unnecessary fear.

For owners wishing to become more comfortable around their injected Alfas, the Alfa club offers some relatively painless methods. Tech clinics, pump teardowns, discussion sessions and the advice of more experienced members are available on a regular basis. While all cars are becoming more complex, very few have this type of extensive support network available to make informed ownership both possible and enjoyable.

The '69 models were instantly recognizable under the hood by their dual brake boosters. The cam cover, once polished to such a high degree of finish, is actually quite easy to keep looking that way. On more than one occasion, concours judges have tried to deduct points for chroming on such cars, and had to be shown that nothing more than elbow grease and enthusiasm had been applied. Author photo.

The 1969 version of the GTV had its front-end styling considerably cleaned up. The front lip of the hood was flushed in and the associated sculpturing in the fenders removed. The grille was reduced to a single bar with mesh background and a four-headlamp system was adopted. The outer seven-inch lamps still provided the usual bright/dim functions, while the new five-inch units served as fog lights. Many owners soon discovered that aircraft landing lights were a bolt-in replacement for the fogs, and gave incredible visibility for nighttime flying on back roads. Also new were the small, round, front and rear sidemarker lamps. Former author vehicle. Author photo.

MODEL: 1750 GTV
BODY TYPE: two-door coupe
BODY DESIGNER: Bertone
WHEELBASE 92.5 in.
TRACK, FRONT: 51.6 in.
REAR: 50.0 in.
WEIGHT: 2288 lbs., Europe; 2325 lbs., U.S.
BRAKES, FRONT: disc
REAR: disc
COMPRESSION RATIO: 9:1
CARBURETION: dual sidedraft Webers, Europe; Spica mechanical injection, U.S.
HORSEPOWER: 118 @ 5500 (135 SAE), Europe; 132 SAE @ 5500 (SAE), U.S.
AXLE RATIO: 9/41 (4.56)

105-Series 1750

ENGINE
Type: In-line four-cylinder
Block: Cast aluminum with slip-fit wet iron liners
Head: Cast aluminum, cross flow, sodium-cooled exhaust valves, hemispherical chambers
Bore x stroke: 80mm x 88.5mm
Displacement: 1779 cc (1750 nominal)
Valve actuation: Chain driven, dual overhead cams, bucket tappets, shim adjustment
DRIVETRAIN
Transmission: Five-speed, Porsche-type synchromesh, aluminum split-case
Clutch: Single-disc with diaphragm pressure plate, hydraulic actuation
Driveshaft: Two-piece with front Metalastic joint, double U-joint, slip spline and center support bearing
Tire size: 165-14
Wheels: 5 1/2 x 14
SUSPENSION
Front: Lower A-arm with upper transverse and longitudinal links, sway bar
Rear: Solid axle with longitudinal radius arms and T-bar locators, sway bar
Shock absorbers: Tubular, hydraulic

Ken Askew's 1971 1750 GTV. The '71's were easy to identify with their larger side-marker lights and taillights, and defroster wires in the rear window. The Cromadora magnesium wheels were very light and had excellent corrosion resistance. Author photo.

When the Alfasud plant opened in Naples in 1972, the Milano reference was dropped from the badge. This version of the emblem, in plastic, has been supplied on all Alfas since then. Author photo.

For the 1750 models, the quadrifoglio badge became gold-on-white, and was not as pleasing as the earlier ivory-and-green emblem of the Giulia. Author photo.

The 1750 GTV's speedometer and tach were housed in large pods molded into the dash top. This is a beautifully configured instrument panel, the best of the 105-Series designs. Author photo.

MODEL: 1750 Spider Veloce
BODY TYPE: two-place roadster
BODY DESIGNER: Pininfarina
WHEELBASE 88.6 in.
TRACK, FRONT: 51.6 in.
      REAR: 50.0 in.
WEIGHT: 2288 lbs., Europe; 2346 lbs., U.S.
BRAKES, FRONT: disc
      REAR: disc
COMPRESSION RATIO: 9:1
CARBURETION: dual sidedraft Webers, Europe; Spica mechanical injection, U.S.
HORSEPOWER: 118 @ 5500 (135 SAE), Europe; 132 SAE @ 5500, U.S.
AXLE RATIO: 10/41 (4.10), Europe; 9/41 (4.56), U.S.

The Spider interior was upgraded to this configuration in 1971 when the square-tail was adopted, and has remained essentially unchanged through the early eighties. The large, round, heavily shrouded instruments conveyed a sense of classic sportiness, and the console was a functional and well-integrated assembly. The vinyl shift boots did not stand up very long to the flexing required and soon developed splits; replacement with a leather boot solved the problem. The defroster was powerful and effective, but the central ducts did not provide good coverage at the outer portions of the windshield. Author photo.

The trunk of an Alfa Spider always amazes onlookers as an owner begins unpacking far more than it seems the car could ever hold. To maintain your dignity when entering the very low seats of the Spider, try backing in and sitting down first, then swinging your feet in the door. If you try to step in first with one foot as many do, you'll find you *fall* the last six inches onto the seat. Author photo.

Mr. Arturo Reitz of Alfa Romeo, Inc., happily showing off his latest wares—the then-new 1750 injected Spider. This was to be the last year for the round-tail or boat-tail design. In 1971, a square-tail configuration that reduced aerodynamic drag was announced. Mr. Reitz, a well-known and respected person among Alfisti, was responsible for the official establishment of ARI in the United States. He had a strong interest in competition, and provided much assistance to owners racing their Alfas. Don Bruno photo.

This well-maintained 1750 Spider owned by Irv and Vivian Wallace was the first fuel-injected Alfa. It is chassis number three, and was used to certify the Spica injection system with the Environmental Protection Agency; the first two cars were destroyed in factory development and crash testing. Author photo.

Another of the "missing" years for Alfa in the U.S. was 1972. When the 1973 models arrived, they featured a larger and more powerful two-liter engine. The extra displacement was obtained by increasing the 80 mm bore of the 1750 to 84 mm while retaining the 88.5 mm stroke. While the European 2000 models retained the 105-Series designation, the U.S. version was reclassified as the 115 Series.

All the 2000 engine crankshafts were nitrided, a surface-hardening process that significantly reduced wear. They had larger intake valves than the 1750 for better breathing, and the old replaceable-element oil filter canister finally gave way to the spin-on type. Both intake and exhaust cams were of milder profile than the 1750 and their timing was changed to reduce overlap.

The only significant chassis change was the addition of a much-needed limited-slip differential. Because of it, the two-liter cars had a definite advantage accelerating out of a low-speed corner. The few 1972 models that were imported from Canada did not have the limited-slip feature. The brakes were also made slightly larger, even though the 1750's would have been more than adequate. The hydraulic clutch slave cylinder design was changed to eliminate the need for periodic adjustment.

The bodywork on all three models remained essentially unchanged, except for trim and instrumentation updates. The 2000 cc Alfas drove and felt much like the 1750 models, but with a noticeable increase in low rpm torque. The bigger engine seemed less willing to rev, however, and its performance was a little disappointing, especially when compared to the 150-SAE-horsepower European version.

Many owners soon discovered that retiming the ignition and cams to 1750 specifications provided the expected power level and boosted gas economy as a bonus. Highway mileage in the mid-thirties was not uncommon for a properly tuned 2000 injected Alfa.

While head gasket failures were an occasional nuisance on the earlier engines, the taller block and cylinder liners seemed to aggravate the condition in the 2000. The differential expansion of the aluminum block and iron liners meant the block would shrink away from the head when cold, leaving the head clamped against the top of the liners. On a cold start, the oil pressure would force its way past the six O-ring seals between the head and block, deteriorating the gasket. When oil appears in the coolant, it's time for a new gasket. When this is done, having the head surfaced, installing roll pins in the oil passages at the top of the block (a factory production fix) and using higher quality Viton O-rings will effectively eliminate this problem.

The new spin-on oil filter must be tightened very securely, or it will vibrate loose. The differential must be filled with lubricant formulated for use with limited slips, or terrible grunching noises will result which fortunately clear up when the correct fluid is supplied. Body corrosion areas must also be monitored.

While the nitrided crank has proven to be nearly indestructible, it will occasionally lose one of the aluminum plugs that are driven in to seal the ends of its drilled oil passages. Although this drops the oil pressure, the engines seem to survive the trauma quite well, even for long periods of time. Of course, immediate repair is desirable and this may actually be done in the car by removing the sump, although a bench repair is highly preferred. A popular and permanent repair involves threading the passages and installing pipe plugs with Loctite, but rebalancing is then necessary.

Don't get the wrong impression—the two-liter injected Alfas are incredibly robust and reliable cars. Like the 1750's, they are everyday usable and as vice-free as an exotic can get. They offer very good value for the money, and parts are not a problem at all.

Berlina

While sharing the same basic bodyshell, the 2000 Berlina was given a revised grille and restyled instrument panel from the 1750 version. It was introduced in Europe in 1971, three years after the 1750 Berlina

Berlina ★
GTV ★★
Spider Veloce ★★

	CHASSIS NUMBERS	
1971-?:	10512.2300001-10512.?	Berlina
1971-1974:	11500.3000001-11500.?	Berlina (U.S.)
1971-?:	10521.2420001-10521.?	GTV
1971-1974:	11501.3020001-11501.?	GTV (U.S.)
1971-?:	10524.2460001-10524.?	Spider Veloce
1971-pres:	11502.3040001-11502.?	Spider Veloce (U.S.)

The 2000 Berlina front end was cleaned up and given a larger grille. The background mesh was cast in plastic to provide much easier maintenance. Author photo.

first appeared. It replaced the 1750 Berlina in the U.S. market in 1973, and was sold for only one more year until it was superceded by the Alfetta sedan in 1975. Production continued for the European market through the late-seventies.

The 2000 Berlina can be considered to be essentially the same car as the 1750 sedan, with some detail refinements and the superior power and torque of the larger engine. If you like the 1750 Berlina, you will find the two-liter version even nicer.

However, it also suffers from the same image problem that has always plagued sales of Alfa sedans in the U.S. Traditional Alfa enthusiasts generally avoid it because it isn't sufficiently sporting, while the typical domestic-car buyer either doesn't know of its existence or avoids it as too exotic. So like the 1750, the 2000 Berlinas are great bargains for the enthusiast needing four doors, but are very hard to sell when you decide to move on to something else.

GTV

Although introduced in Europe in 1971 and continued into the late-seventies, the 2000 GTV was available in the U.S. for only two model years, 1973 and 1974, and then as a replacement for the 1750 coupe. For both those years there were no significant changes in appearance.

Compared to the 1750, the newer GTV featured a revised and somewhat less attractive instrument cluster with plastic rather than glass lenses. The seats were carried over from the 1971 coupe, the center console was restyled, and a wooden-rim steering wheel added. Externally, the grillework was redone and gave a much busier, almost out-of-focus, look to the front end. The C-pillar emblem became an attractive, stylized cast-metal part.

In 1973, an enlarged fourteen-gallon gas tank was provided that was highly desirable for its extra range despite the slight encroachment on trunk space. Strangely, the smaller 12.5-gallon tank was reinstated for 1974.

Generally, the 2000 GTV's feel much like their 1750 predecessors, with the main differences being the extra torque of the larger engine and the advantage of a limited-slip differential. They are usually priced slightly higher than the 1750's for no other reason than that they are several years newer.

Asking prices have held up reasonably well, reflecting the high regard in which the 105-Series Bertone coupes are held. Many prefer them to the larger Alfetta coupes that followed, and well-preserved examples should always retain a high value in the future. As the last of the many variations of this model, the 2000 GTV is not only the most highly developed but also is the fastest and easiest to drive. It is a handsome, classic GT that will be long remembered as one of Alfa's most satisfying production designs.

Spider Veloce

Introduced in 1971 along with the coupe and sedan, the 2000 Spider Veloce has proven to be the survivor of the three models and remains in production as of this writing. The U.S. 115-Series version was equipped with Spica mechanical fuel injection and was not brought in until 1973, when it replaced the 1750 roadster. The body and chassis were unchanged, and the only way to tell the two versions apart was to look for the 2000 script over the taillight.

The Spider benefited from the extra torque of the two-liter engine even more than the other models because of its weight advantage. Its slippery shape also allowed impressive acceleration at any speed, and the limited-slip unit gave a very strong, competent feel while powering out of a hard turn.

Problem areas are not much different than those experienced with the 1750 model. Corrosion remains a major concern, primarily in the rocker panel structure and wheelwells. The small drain hole in the spare tire well must be kept open or water will be trapped, eventually ruining both the tire well and the spare wheel. All soft tops inevitably leak, so inspect under the floor mats and behind and under the seats after a heavy rain.

The Spider has padding glued to the floorpan on the inside to reduce noise and exhaust heat, but once wet, the padding will retain the water for a long time and rust out the floor from the inside. If you live in a wet region and find yourself continually drying out the floor padding, it may be best to scrape it off, clean and repaint the floor sheetmetal and install replaceable insulation. The later Spiders with carpeting present a special problem, and the best approach is to simply work on minimizing the leakage.

The square-tail Spiders have a drain trough around the lower perimeter of the soft top with four drain tubes that empty down into the rocker panel area. These drain tube outlets are easily sealed shut when a Spider is undercoated and the trough will then overflow onto the platform behind the seats and spill over under the seats. Most owners discover this problem during a hard stop, as several

MODEL: Alfetta Sedan/Sport Sedan
BODY TYPE: four-door sedan
BODY DESIGNER: factory
WHEELBASE 98.8
TRACK, FRONT: 53.5 in.
        REAR: 53.2 in.
WEIGHT: 2332 lbs. (1779 cc engine)
        2398 lbs. (2000 cc engine)
BRAKES, FRONT: disc
        REAR: disc (inboard)
COMPRESSION RATIO: 9:1
CARBURETION: dual sidedraft Webers or Dell'Ortos, Europe;
        Spica mechanical injection, U.S.
HORSEPOWER: 118 SAE @ 5500 (1779 engine), 140 SAE @ 5300
        (2000 engine), 111 SAE @ 5000 (2000 engine, U.S. spec.)
AXLE RATIO: 10/41 (4.10)

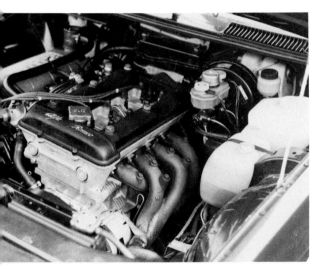

This is the highly regarded European Alfetta exhaust system. It provides a noticeable boost in performance and a three-to-four-mpg fuel economy improvement. Note also that the air pump and heat riser tubes are gone, the air-box inlet is the older 105 style, and the cam cover is from a Giulia. Author photo.

This is as close to a stock Alfetta engine compartment as you are likely to find. The air-conditioning compressor and associated bracketry greatly complicate all maintenance operations at the front of the engine. Author photo.

116-Series Alfetta

ENGINE
Type: In-line four-cylinder
Block: Cast aluminum with slip-fit wet iron liners
Head: Cast aluminum, cross flow, sodium cooled exhaust valves, hemispherical chambers
Bore x stroke: 84mm x 88.5mm
Displacement: 1962 cc (2000 nominal)
Valve actuation: Chain driven, dual overhead cams, bucket tappets, shim adjustment

DRIVETRAIN
Transmission: Five-speed, Porsche-type synchromesh, rear transaxle
Clutch: Single-disc in transaxle with diaphragm pressure plate, hydraulic actuation
Driveshaft: Two-piece with three Metalastic joints and center support bearing
Tire size: 165-14 and 185/70-14
Wheels: 5 1/2 x 14 steel or alloy rims, 6 x 14 alloy rims optional

SUSPENSION
Front: Lower A-arm with upper transverse arm and longitudinal link, sway bar, torsion bar springs
Rear: De Dion axle with lateral locating links, sway bar and coil springs
Shock absorbers: Tubular, hydraulic

The bold, side protective trim and reworked front end gave the Sport Sedan a stylish flair the earlier Alfetta version never had. Virtually all Sport Sedans were equipped with alloy wheels. Author photo.

MODEL: Alfetta GT, GTV, Sprint Veloce
BODY TYPE: two-door coupe
BODY DESIGNER: Bertone
WHEELBASE 94.5
TRACK, FRONT: 53.5 in.
          REAR: 53.5 in.
WEIGHT: 2200 lbs. (1600 cc engine), 2310 lbs. (1779 cc engine),
    2200 lbs. (2000 cc engine), 2660 lbs. (U.S. version)
BRAKES, FRONT: disc
          REAR: disc (inboard)
COMPRESSION RATIO: 9:1
CARBURETION: dual sidedraft Webers or Dell'Ortos, Europe;
    Spica mechanical injection, U.S.
HORSEPOWER: 109 DIN @ 5600 (1600 engine), 122 DIN @ 5500
    (1779 engine), 122 DIN @ 5300 (2000 engine), 111 SAE @ 5000
    (2000 engine, U.S. spec.)
AXLE RATIO: 10/43 (4.30), 1600 cc engine; 10/41 (4.10), all
    others

The Sprint Veloce was primarily a name-change for marketing reasons. The metal framing around the front and rear windows was a major corrosion area. The clips that held down the moldings tended to cut through the paint and allow rust to begin spreading. At the first sign of trouble, the moldings should be removed and the paint repaired. The damage in the trough around the glass can be more extensive than is immediately obvious externally. Filling the trough with a tarlike undercoating substance will prevent recurrence. Author photo.

The 1975 Alfetta GT was identified by the script on the rear hatch. Body panels were not as tightly fitted as on the older models, shown here by the typically wide and variable spacing around the hatch. Author photo.

The 1976 version was called the GTV, which causes occasional confusion with the earlier 105- and 115-Series coupes. The front plastic spoilers are rarely found undamaged, especially on cars that have been lowered. The extreme tuck-under of the rocker and rear quarter-panels makes it advisable to install mud flaps or apply some type of vinyl chip protection to these areas. Former author vehicle. Author photo.

Coupes of 1978 and later acquired a bold, side protective strip and retained the Sprint Veloce designation. The biggest single improvement was the switch to a rubber mounting for the windshield, significantly reducing the corrosion problem of the earlier versions. Author photo.

The Velocissima was a special edition of the Sprint Veloce consisting of add-on aerodynamic aids. The roof deflector, rear spoiler, extractors over the rear vent, wheelwell flairs and large front air dam gave the car a dramatically changed appearance. Author photo.

The new series of V-6 Alfa Romeos was first introduced in 1979 as a large, luxury four-door sedan. Its engine was carbureted with six downdraft throats nestled between the heads. A conventional front five-speed transmission and live rear axle drivetrain was used. A Bosch L-Jetronic fuel-injection version was shown in mid-1980, which was scheduled for the U.S. market. The car is still on display at ARI in New Jersey.

Unfortunately, a timely market study revealed that Americans who even recognized Alfa Romeo as a car manufacturer almost exclusively identified it as a maker of sporting vehicles. This explained Alfa's long-standing difficulty in selling excellent sedans in the U.S.—they just didn't fit the expected exoticar image.

Immediate action was taken. The four-cylinder Sports Sedan was withdrawn from the market, plans to import the big V-6 sedan were scrapped, and development of a performance-oriented V-6 coupe began. The resulting GTV6 became available as a 1981 model, introduced amid the ravings of a delighted and impressed enthusiast press. However, *Road & Track* opinion later cooled on the car and its testers declared it to be a "harsh mistress," after experiencing maintenance difficulties.

For 1986, a new V-6 Sports Sedan was introduced on the GTV6 chassis. Known as the 75 in Europe, to commemorate Alfa's seventy-fifth anniversary, the U.S. version was named the Milano. It had been significantly reconfigured to appeal to American tastes. Initial sales were as good as the press reviews, and surprisingly the Milano was being purchased by longtime owners as well as the first-time owner it was designed to attract, possibly reflecting the seven-year U.S. drought of Alfa sedans.

The V-6 engine maintained the Alfa tradition of being a visual as well as a mechanical delight. The block, sump, heads and cam covers were the usual beautiful aluminum castings. Wet iron liners were again used, as in the four-cylinder engines. Individual tuned-length cast-aluminum runners extended from the air plenum to the intake of each cylinder. The sixty-degree angle between banks gave it considerable width, but provided smooth, vibration-free operation.

The single overhead cams driven by a toothed fiberglass belt represented a significant departure from Alfa's expected twin-cam, chain-drive approach. Each cam acted directly upon the intake valves, but operated the exhaust valves through a lifter and rocker-arm mechanism. It's a very interesting design that preserved the staggered valve configuration and associated excellent cross-flow breathing of a twin-cam, but with reduced cost, weight and bulk.

Engine problem areas have proven to be leaking oil seals in the head gaskets (which are claimed to be fixed in the Milano), water pump bearings at about 40,000 miles, leaking and/or seized cam drive-belt hydraulic tensioner (reassemble the tensioner pivot with silicon grease to eliminate varnishing), and an occasional tendency to throw the alternator/water pump V-belt at high rpm (maintain the belt in good condition and tension).

The Bosch electronic fuel injection provided an excellent balance between the usually conflicting requirements of emissions, power output and driveability. The operation was sufficiently vice-free that it could be favorably compared with pre-emission performance, and has been extremely reliable in the V-6 to date.

The V-6 has already appeared in other applications, including a Zagato coupe and the striking Delfino coupe by Bertone. A number of U.S. carmakers are evaluating the engine for specialty performance applications, and it was even considered by Delorean as an upgrade for his V-6 Renault-powered car. To show its potential, a twin-turbo GTV6 by Calloway with over 200 horsepower was sold as a limited edition through the official dealer network.

119-Series GTV6

Introduced as a 1981 model, the new GTV6 was the first tangible reassurance of Alfa Romeo's renewed commitment to the performance car market. After the Montreal had been discontinued in 1977, there

Although almost entirely based on Alfetta sheetmetal, the GTV6 emerged with a distinct and formidable personality of its own. The hood bulge required to clear the larger engine lent a "muscle car" effect, and the diminutive grille was reminiscent of that used on the Tipo 33 race cars. Author photo.

had been no top-of-the-line "image" car for the company, and the GTV6 was targeted to fill this void.

Superficially, it would be easy to dismiss the GTV6 as an Alfetta GT with a larger engine shoe-horned in. The fact is, it was a totally re-engineered car that merely shared the Alfetta's sheet metal as a production and economic expedient. The entire chassis—wheels and tires, brakes, transaxle, drive-shaft, suspension and overall stiffness—was upgraded to handle the power of the larger engine.

The instrument panel was revised, finally eliminating past Alfetta complaints by locating all gauges in front of the driver. The carpeting quality was improved, extra sound-proofing and power windows were added, all upholstery was done in leather and air conditioning became standard.

Several special editions were produced: the Balocco, the Martona and the Calloway. With the exception of the twin-turbo Calloway, these were basically trim packages on otherwise stock vehicles.

The hood acquired a bulge to clear the air plenum of the V-6. The exterior trim was revised to upgrade the appearance of the car with black-out trim and new plastic panels protecting the wheelwell and rocker panel areas from stone chips. However, the rocker trim does tend to trap dirt and moisture, which then promote rust, and should have drain holes scalloped along the bottom edge for drainage.

Driving a GTV6 is always an eye-opening experience for an Alfetta owner who thinks it is simply a faster version of his own car. It rides and handles better than an Alfetta equipped with after-market performance suspension. The increased rigidity of the body is immediately obvious, providing a rock-solid feel. It soon entices any driver into swooping through high-speed turns and accelerating hard just to hear the beautiful wail of the engine. The effect is much like a U.S. musclecar, except for the refinement and silkiness of the controls, and that wonderful full-throttle engine sound the V-6 provides.

Unlike the Alfetta, the GTV6 is set up exactly the way an enthusiast driver would want, and is a most satisfying sports GT in completely stock form. For those desiring slightly less understeer, a heavier rear swaybar is all that's needed. In fact, the U.S. and European versions are essentially identical, with both using the Bosch L-Jetronic fuel-injection system. The few extra horsepower of the European car results primarily from additional distributor advance.

Despite its performance orientation and good value for the dollar, the GTV6 has proven to be a difficult car to sell in the U.S. market, either new or used, resulting in fairly rapid depreciation. This offers a real opportunity for bargain hunters, as early GTV6's can often be found for economy car prices. That's unfortunate and undeserved, as the GTV6 is a much better car than this situation implies. If it is ever discontinued without an immediate replacement, prices should recover to more reasonable levels.

161-Series Milano

Introduced in the summer of 1986, the Milano sedan was an instant hit with the enthusiast press as well as with owners who snapped them up as fast as they could be supplied. The large number of Milanos that showed up at the 1986 Alfa Club national meet right after their introduction was a surprise to all, and indicated that Alfa's marketing was right on target with this model.

Three versions were offered—the Silver, the Gold and the Platinum Quadrifoglio—which featured increasing levels of luxury and technology. The Silver Quadrifoglio was as basic as the U.S. Milano, and the closest to the European version. It had 14×5.5-inch steel wheels, fabric upholstery and optional air conditioning.

The Gold version upgraded to 5.5×14 alloy wheels, power antenna, side mirrors and power velour sport seats heated for the driver.

The top-of-the-line Platinum Quadrifoglio brought 6×15 alloy wheels and performance 205/55-15 tires, air conditioning, standard sunroof, limited slip differential and leather interior with heated driver seat. Another first, ABS brakes, provided electronic skid control which should be phenomenal given the Milano's already excellent four-wheel disc system.

All versions had another Alfa first—power steering. It was designed to have minimal effect at speed to maintain good road feel, yet give assist for low-speed parking maneuvers. Despite lots of the traditional Alfa body roll in hard cornering, the Milano was very pleasing and crisp to drive, and acquit itself well in autocrossing, an unexpected bonus for a luxury-oriented sedan.

The interior represented a major philosophical shift from past Alfa practice and was highly detailed and nicely appointed, in contrast to the expected sporty functionality. Controls and switches abounded for all the power options, and the overall effect suggested both American and Japanese influence. An adjustable steering column allowed fore-aft as well as tilt adjustment. Features never before contemplated for an Alfa were offered: power locking doors, power seat tracks, stereo headset

Series V-6

ENGINE
Type: Six-cylinder Vee
Block: Cast aluminum with slip-fit wet iron liners
Head: Cast aluminum, cross flow, sodium cooled exhaust valves, hemispherical chambers
Bore x stroke: 84mm x 88.5mm
Displacement: 1962 cc (2500 nominal)
Valve actuation: Fiberglass cog-belt driven single overhead cams, bucket tappets on intakes, rockers on exhausts
DRIVETRAIN
Transmission: Five-speed, Porsche-type synchromesh, rear transaxle
Clutch: Twin-disc in transaxle, diaphragm pressure plate, hydraulic actuation
Driveshaft: Two-piece with three Metalastic joints and center support bearing
Tire size: 195/60-15
Wheels: 6 x 15 alloy rims
SUSPENSION
Front: Lower A-arm with upper transverse arm and longitudinal link, sway bar, torsion bar springs
Rear: De Dion axle with lateral locating links, sway bar and coil springs
Shock absorbers: Tubular, hydraulic

The magnificent new V-6 engine came as a total surprise in an era when emission requirements and economics were forcing ever cheapened and strangled designs. It was an absolute gift to the enthusiast driver. The Bosch L-Jetronic fuel injection gave nearly vice-free operation with excellent power output and good fuel economy. Author photo.

The taillights of the GTV6 were one-piece units with greatly reduced tendency to cause rust problems in the surrounding sheetmetal. The new rear plastic extractor vents hinted at the Tipo 33-based Carabo show car. Author vehicle.

jacks and high-output air conditioning. The seats were comfortable, but the interior was a little tight for a six-footer.

A three-liter engine is promised for later, as well as an automatic transmission option. This will be available on yet another version—the Green Quadrifoglio—which promises to be the performance edition.

The parking-brake handle had a clever new design concept. Its U shape, although tunnel mounted, did not intrude on the useful top area of the console, and its front crossbar provided for a secure grip and allowed a hefty pull to be applied.

Access to the front of the engine with the rear-opening hood was far easier than on the GTV6, and greatly simplified servicing of all the front belt-driven accessories. The driveline was essentially identical to the coupe, with improvements to the transaxle and shift linkage that should minimize previous complaints of vagueness.

The overall styling was crisp, modern and attractive, with only one discordant note—the broken upsweep in the side trim that emphasized the high rear quarter and made it appear bent. This has inspired typical tongue-in-cheek Alfa humor about bodyshops encountering their first crunched Milano and attempting in vain to straighten the trunk. Yet this high tail did provide a spacious luggage compartment, despite the intrusion of the rear transaxle and DeDion suspension links, so it was functional and beneficial. The front end had aerodynamic flush-mounted halogen headlights, part of the Milano's 130 mph capability.

The Milano was really the first vehicle Alfa configured specifically for the U.S. market, and with it the company intended to penetrate the status sport sedan category with annual sales approaching 10,000 vehicles. To attract and hold this new type of Alfa buyer, a factory final inspection program was used to ensure defect-free cars. A three-year/36,000-mile warranty was provided and extendable to six years/60,000 miles, and comprehensive delivery and follow-up programs were planned to increase owner satisfaction. Efforts have been made to eliminate those little nuisance items that traditional owners merely found amusing or overlooked. A good example is the replacement of the older-style troublesome fuse box with modern plug-in fuses, particularly important with all the electronic systems on board that require good continuity.

Eight-second 0-60 times, the long list of desirable features, good press and a bargain entry-level price of $12,900 in 1986 will ensure the Milano is at least considered by many potential new buyers looking for a four-door performance car. If sales live up to expectations, the Milano will be the first Alfa sedan to eclipse the sales of its counterpart coupe and roadster models in this market, and will be the springboard to a greater Alfa presence in the U.S. in the future.

The standard 195/60-15 Pirelli P-6 tires on 6X15 alloy rims left little doubt as to the high-performance orientation of the GTV6. Author photo.

```
MODEL: GTV6
BODY TYPE: two-door coupe
BODY DESIGNER: Bertone
WHEELBASE 94.5
TRACK, FRONT: 53.5 in.
        REAR: 53.5 in.
WEIGHT: 2840 lbs.
BRAKES, FRONT: disc
        REAR: disc (inboard)
COMPRESSION RATIO: 9.1:1
CARBURETION: Bosch L-Jetronic injection
HORSEPOWER: 154 SAE @ 5500 rpm
AXLE RATIO: 4.10, 1981; 3.42, 1982 and later
```

The interior of the GTV6 featured all-leather up-holstery, high-quality, fine-textured carpeting and a very businesslike instrument panel. Author photo.

The Balocco Special Edition was a limited-quantity variation of the GTV6 named after Alfa Romeo's proving ground. This was primarily a trim package with external striping and darkened wheel centers and some interior upholstery changes. Author photo.

A conservative yet distinctive appearance, high performance without racy lines or flame decals, and elegance and quality without sticker shock make the Milano a difficult car to categorize or ignore. Dave Hammond photo.

The V-6 engine undergoing development tests on the dynamometer. Factory photo.

The color of the quadrifoglio above the taillight is the quickest indicator of Milano trim level—silver, gold, platinum or (by 1987) green. Be careful of cars that have been "upgraded" by a simple emblem change. Dave Hammond photo.

Three Milanos in a row highlight the modern low-nose, high-tail wedge styling. The small protrusions on the bumper house spray nozzles for washing the aero headlights. Dave Hammond photo.

On the Calloway twin-turbo GTV6, the functional hood scoop feeds cooling air to the intercooler. Other than fancy wheels, the chassis is perfectly stock and adequately handles a 45-percent power boost. Dave Hammond photo.

CHAPTER 16
MONTREAL

For the 1967 World's Fair in Montreal, Alfa Romeo was asked to provide an exhibit as a representative of the automobile industry. The response was an interesting prototype designed in collaboration with Bertone, and named the Montreal in honor of the event. Based heavily on the 105-Series chassis components and obviously designed with the possibility of eventual production in mind, it generated considerable interest and a lot of inquiries. Many thought it would be the replacement for the Giulia GTV.

When the production version finally was shown in 1970, its styling differed only in minor detailing from the original; the real surprise was under the hood. In a rather dramatic gesture, Alfa powered the new car with the Type 33 race car four-cam V-8 engine. Detuned for the street, this impressive powerplant still managed a 230-SAE-horsepower output from only 2593 cc displacement. Once again, here was Alfa's competition-derived equipment turned loose for everyday use.

Fuel was supplied by Spica mechanical injection. A unit very similar to that used for emissions tuning on the four-cylinder cars was modified to provide the extra four fuel outlets required by the V-8, plus the fuel-delivery curve was reworked. Ram tubes inside the air cleaner box tuned the intake to optimize cylinder filling as on the four-cylinder engines.

The production chassis was still based on 105-Series mechanicals, including the familiar solid rear axle setup, showing the real potential and inherent over-design of these excellent components. Despite the extra bulk of the engine and the larger size of the vehicle itself, the Montreal weighed in at only 2,800 pounds. The transmission was a five-speed design—regrettably not the Type 33's six-speed, a result of not using the race car's transaxle.

The interior was very nicely done, with quite large and comprehensive gauges on the instrument panel. There were enough borrowed hardware and trim items to make a 105-Series owner smile with recognition. The view over the seemingly flat hood was considerably nicer and more contoured than would be expected from the outside. The Montreal was far more beautiful in person than most people expected from photos. The car had some nicely executed bulges and contours on its flanks, particularly around the functional side air vents, that were very difficult to capture with a camera. It came across on paper as very slab-sided and less interesting than it really was.

There were even more surprises waiting when you drove a Montreal. The first was the hefty steering; this was not a car for tight parking maneuvers. The next was the engine sound—a well-muffled but very busy collection of precision thrashings and clickings, with electric-drill smoothness and docile response.

Winding up to what sounded like a good shift-point, the Montreal would turn in a reasonably strong performance. But a glance at the tach revealed only around 4000 rpm—the car hadn't even begun to show its potential. With its fairly tall gearing, firm ride and heavy camber, the Montreal was obviously intended as a high-speed contender for the Autostrada.

Although never certified to U.S. standards, Montreals seem to be appearing here in ever increasing numbers as individuals privately import them. Most appear to be in very good condition, showing a high level of care and regard by their owners. While prices vary somewhat, they are usually in the same range as a new Alfa coupe. Parts are surprisingly available in the U.S. for such a limited-production car that was never brought in by the factory. For the enthusiast looking for a large, powerful and impressive GT with traditional Alfa qualities, the Montreal is an excellent choice and a potentially good investment.

CHASSIS NUMBERS
1971-197?:   10564.1425101-10564.?——The Montreal

The detailing at the rear was somewhat busy, but the Kamm-effect
square-tail was aerodynamically effective. Author photo.

105-Series Montreal

ENGINE

Type: V-8

Block: Cast aluminum with slip-fit wet iron liners

Head: Cast aluminum, cross flow, sodium cooled exhaust valves, hemispherical chambers

Bore x stroke: 80mm x 64.5mm

Displacement: 2593 cc (2600 nominal)

Valve actuation: Chain driven, dual overhead cams, bucket tappets, shim adjustment

DRIVETRAIN

Transmission: Five-speed, Porsche-type synchromesh, aluminum split-case

Clutch: Single-disc with diaphragm pressure plate, hydraulic actuation

Driveshaft: Two-piece with front Metalastic joint, double U-joint, slip spline and center support bearing

Tire size: 195/70 VR 14

Wheels: 14-inch alloy rims

SUSPENSION

Front: Lower A-arm with upper transverse and longitudinal links, sway bar

Rear: Solid axle with longitudinal radius arms and T-bar locators, sway bar

Shock absorbers: Tubular, hydraulic

Author departing for a test drive in Ken Wears' rapid Montreal. Ken Wears photo.

Bill Hardy's much-photographed and immaculate Montreal is frequently displayed with a mirror under the front grille. This allows passers-by to admire the spotlessly clean undercarriage and polished suspension members. Author photo.

Two giant pods on the Montreal instrument panel housed a multitude of gauges. Jeanette Benson photo.

MODEL: Montreal
BODY TYPE: two-door coupe
BODY DESIGNER: Bertone
WHEELBASE 92.5 in.
TRACK, FRONT: 54.0 in.
         REAR: 52.8
WEIGHT: 2794 lbs.
BRAKES, FRONT: disc
          REAR: disc
COMPRESSION RATIO: 9.3:1
CARBURETION: Spica mechanical injection
HORSEPOWER: 230 SAE @ 6500 rpm
AXLE RATIO: 10/41 (4.10)

The four overhead cams of the Montreal V-8 gave an illusion of much greater engine size than the actual 2.6 liters. The ram tubes inside the air cleaner tuned the intake passages for strong mid-range torque. Author photo.

Alfa Romeo's primary market is Italy, of course. The Common Market countries in Europe logically come next, with the highest sales in Germany. In fact, Alfa owners frequently gloat about Alfa out-selling Porsche in its home country. Out of fairness though, the vehicles involved are in completely different price classes, plus Porsche tends to deliberately tailor its cars for export purposes.

The farther one ventures from Europe, the more restricted the choice of models generally becomes, and not only from Alfa. Because of differing regulations and the logistics of maintaining remote sales and parts networks, most European car companies sell only selected vehicles that have the best chance of success in foreign markets. The U.S. is one of the most difficult places for such manufacturers because of its complex regulations, and some companies, like Citroen and Morgan, have simply decided it isn't worth the trouble and expense.

Up through the mid-sixties, Alfa's vehicle selection was sufficiently small that Americans could choose from any of the European models; they were all available here. The U.S. safety and emission standards coincided with Alfa's expansion into a greater number of model lines, and forced a decision to limit U.S. certification to a single series at any given time.

This has had the effect of providing a small, restrictive "window" through which Americans have been able to view the company and its products. So while it seemed that Alfa's models were logically progressing from the Giulias to the 1750 to the 2000 to the Alfetta and finally to the V-6, the European picture was far more complex. Virtually all these vehicles were available simultaneously, with a few extras thrown in such as the Alfasud, the new Giulietta and the Montreal.

The full extent of Alfa's European offerings is not at all appreciated in the U.S. Even regular readers of the enthusiast publications receive only a slim notion of Alfa's diversity. Avid Alfisti stay much more in touch through sales literature and club newsletter articles, but then typically become frustrated over the wide selection of desirable Alfas denied them. Keep in mind as you peruse this chapter that only the GTV6 and Spider Veloce are presently certified for sale here, and you will begin to understand the enthusiast's unhappiness.

1300 Giulias

In 1964, two years after the 1600 Giulia series was announced, a smaller-displacement version was offered based on the new sedan. Known as the Giulia 1300 Berlina, it utilized the Giulietta engine with single downdraft Solex carburetor. It produced 78 CV horsepower. Although discontinued in 1966, it was replaced by the Giulia 1300 T.I., a slightly higher performance version with 82 CV or 94 SAE horsepower.

A coupe version was also introduced that year based on the Giulia Sprint G.T. It was not until 1968 that the 1300 version of the Spider appeared. These were known respectively as the GT 1300 Junior and the Spider 1300 Junior. Both came with a somewhat higher engine output of 103 SAE horsepower and dual sidedraft Weber carburetors.

The interior and exterior trim of these 1300 Giulia vehicles was simplified from the 1600 cc versions. The sedan and coupe reverted to single headlamps with much plainer front ends. The coupe and roadster did not have the consoles of their larger-displacement cousins. In some, the steering wheels were even reduced to two-spoke arrangements.

The 1300 Giulias' prime attractions were their lower initial cost, improved fuel economy and a favorable tax category, which in Europe is steeply graduated and generally based on displacement. They opened the possibility of Alfa ownership to many who could otherwise not have afforded it. In all, 172,571 sedans, 80,623 coupes and 4,538 roadsters were built. The 1300 Giulia series was discontinued in 1972 with the introduction of the Alfasud, which fit the same market requirements.

A few 1300 Giulias have managed to find their way into the U.S. Because of the significantly different fuel costs, vehicle tax system and driving conditions here, the economic advantage of the

1300 Giulia ★★
New Giulietta ★★
Diesel ★★
V-6 Sedan ★★
Alfasud ★★

CHASSIS NUMBERS
1966-1972: 10539.621001-10539.761245——1300 T.I.
1966-1972: 10530.1200101-10530.1276072——G.T. 1300 Junior
1968-1972: 10591.1670001-10591.1674360——Spider 1300 Junior
CHASSIS NUMBERS
1972-pres: AS 5000001-?——Alfasud Berlina 4-Dr

The single seven-inch headlights mark this Giulia sedan as a 1300.
Author photo.

smaller engine is completely lost. In fact, this is one of the few examples where the European version of an Alfa provides lower performance than the U.S. specification cars and is therefore not as desirable. This is reflected in the price when a 1300 Giulia does come up for sale—it generally brings slightly less than a comparable 1600 or 1750 version and attracts fewer potential buyers.

Alfasud

The new front-wheel-drive Alfasud sedan was first shown at Turin in 1971, and became available for sale in 1972. An excellent design, it broke Alfa tradition in many respects. Forsaking the evolutionary approach of the other models, it boasted an entirely new engine, driveline and body shape. If it were not for the familiar heart-shaped Alfa grille, it would be almost impossible for even a knowledgeable Alfa enthusiast to recognize its origins without being told.

The Alfasud was most impressive to drive. It was immensely quiet and smooth, and would easily absorb the shock of potholes that would seriously ruffle the composure of the "larger" Alfas. Its excellent handling characteristics, helped by a low-center-of-gravity engine, made the Alfasud nearly the equal of the 1750 and 2000 cars on the track, despite its 1186 cc displacement.

Its drivetrain featured a boxer four-cylinder, water-cooled engine with belt-driven single-overhead cams producing 73 SAE horsepower, Alfa's first postwar design to abandon the twin-overhead-cam approach. The front four-speed transaxle was later upgraded to provide a more satisfying five-speed unit. Shifting was very precise, thanks to a rigid extension of the transaxle to which the shift lever attached.

A year later the T.I. version was introduced with an extra six horsepower and sportier appointments. In 1975 a Giardinetta, or station wagon, was added. But the real treat came in 1974 with the long-awaited announcement of the coupe version—the Alfasud Sprint. It featured a larger 1286 cc engine with 87 SAE horsepower and styling reminiscent of the Alfetta GT, but smaller and crisper.

Since then, a 1500 version has also been announced, and a variety of performance variations of both sedan and coupe have appeared.

Alfasuds unfortunately soon developed a reputation for rusting. Alfa responded by specifying a high percentage of zinc-coated sheetmetal, foam-filling the rocker structures and other cavities, and improving the paint and antichip coatings. As a result, the Alfasud was transformed into one of the most corrosion-resistant small cars in the industry.

If the vehicle was unconventional, the politics behind it were even stranger. The Italian government, as part of its effort to industrialize Southern Italy, directed Alfa to locate its new plant in Naples. The very name Alfasud reflected this, translating simply as "Alfa-south." Although there was considerable resistance at first, Alfa eventually complied and solved the problem of having an unskilled workforce by introducing a very high level of automation. Smooth labor relations were another matter, and the Alfasud plant was plagued with constant ministrikes, rumored to have reached as many as a thousand one year.

Things are a little more settled now than in those early days, but Alfasud production has never consistently attained the high levels originally envisioned. In fact, it was a surplus production capacity of Alfasud engines that prompted Alfa to enter into an agreement in 1982 with Nissan for joint manufacture of a new small front-drive vehicle under the ARNA designation. It was discontinued in 1986.

At present, there are no known Alfasuds in the U.S., but that doesn't mean a few haven't sneaked in unnoticed. As for price, it would be purely a matter of vehicle condition and the negotiating skills of the owner and prospective buyer. It's really unfortunate that Alfa has chosen not to sell the Alfasud here, for it would not only appeal to its traditional customers, but could also introduce many others to Alfa's enthusiastic approach to transportation.

New Giulietta

Once again Alfa reached into its own past to name a new model. However, with the new Giulietta sedan, very little rationale could be found to connect it with the original except the availability of a 1300 cc engine. Its chassis was so obviously Alfetta-derived, with a front twin-cam engine, rear clutch, transaxle and DeDion axle, that it would be more realistic to think of it as another version of the Alfetta sedan.

The styling was somewhat on the strange side, yet still managed to be interesting. The high tail contributed to a wedge styling effect, plus provided excellent trunk capacity and good aerodynamics. The new Giulietta offered the same superb ride and handling characteristics of the Alfetta vehicles.

Like the Alfasud, the early new Giuliettas developed a reputation for rust problems. In a similar manner, Alfa combined the use of zinc-coated sheetmetal with improved sealers and paints to virtually eliminate the corrosion difficulties.

The rear script reveals this is the more powerful T.I. version. The taillights are also the smallest of the three different units used on the Giulia sedan series. Author photo.

A 1500 T.I. with a "whale-tail" rear spoiler based on the two-door sedan. Mike Hemsley photo.

Also like the Alfasud, there are few, if any, known new Giuliettas in the U.S., so there isn't much need to worry about their pricing.

Diesel

In response to the fuel crises of the early seventies, the Giulia Nuova Super—the updated Giulia Super sedan—was fitted in 1976 with a Perkins Diesel engine of 1760 cc producing 55 SAE horsepower. Approximately 6,500 of these cars were built.

A better solution was found later when Alfa discovered that Stabilimenti Meccanici VM, one of its associates in the government IRI group, was producing an excellent 1995 cc, four-cylinder automotive turbo-diesel. It featured relatively high rpm capability, impressive output of 83 horsepower plus relatively light weight. It also fit quite well into the Alfetta sedan and detracted far less from the sporting character than the earlier Perkins approach.

In 1982, a high-performance version fitted with a Comprex supercharger was shown. Its performance reportedly was a very respectable 0-60 in twelve seconds with a top speed of 108 mph, while delivering 32.6 mpg city and 47.2 mpg highway during EPA testing.

At this writing, there are no plans to market a diesel Alfa in the U.S., but that could easily change if there is another protracted fuel shortage.

V-6 Sedan

A large, luxurious, four-door sedan was the first vehicle to be fitted with Alfa's new V-6 engine. In European trim it was equipped with a cluster of six carburetor throats, one per cylinder, nestled compactly between the vee-banks. In 1980, a Bosch fuel-injected version was shown that was intended for the U.S., with a projected price in the mid-twenties. However, it was about that time that Alfa reevaluated its U.S. marketing strategy and decided an expensive sedan was the wrong approach.

This was especially true of the V-6 sedan, with its deliberately bland appearance. While the inconspicuous approach had a great deal of antikidnap value in the home market, it would be very difficult to sell to style-conscious Americans.

Those who have driven the V-6 sedan have nothing but praise for its comfort level and performance. A few of these large Alfas have found their way into the U.S. Parts should not be too serious a problem because of many shared pieces with the GTV6. Establishing a price would be mere guesswork, but a comparable GTV6 could certainly be used as a minimum basis.

Alfa 33

The Alfa Type 33 was introduced in 1983 as an upgraded replacement for the Alfasud sedan. Based on the same Alfasud driveline, it was the first Alfa to feature the kick-up side trim at the tail that would later be used on the 75 or Milano. A four-wheel-drive wagon version utilizing Subaru components is offered, and is the first road Alfa to be so configured.

U.S. Available Models

All the Alfa models sold in the U.S. were also available in Europe, although not always in the same trim. Up through 1967, there was no real difference in either availability or specification of Alfas for the home market and the U.S. After 1967, the U.S. regulations brought about many limitations on what Alfas Americans could buy.

But even the models that remained available here were considerably different than the European versions. In general, the European Alfas were lighter and more powerful than their U.S. counterparts, and thus notably faster. One result was a widespread tendency among American owners to "upgrade" their Alfas to the more-performance-oriented European components. But instead of enhancing the value, such modifications frequently made it difficult or impossible to register a car, and could thus reduce its desirability.

The water-cooled, boxer four of the Alfasud sat quite low in the chassis. This is one of the perform- ance versions with a dual-throat carb bolted directly to each head. Mike Hemsley photo.

The front of the T.I. showed a sizeable air dam and an atypical quad headlamp treatment. If the Alfasud is ever brought into the U.S., it will most likely be in this configuration. Mike Hemsley photo.

Plexiglas headlamp covers on the European Spiders completed the rounded fender line in the manner Pininfarina originally intended. The shallow front bumpers gave a much lighter look to the nose, but made it even more susceptible to parking damage. Mike Hemsley photo.

The special Plus version of the Giugiaro-designed Alfasud Sprint coupe. Mike Hemsley photo.

Here the continuity of the Giulietta's wedge shape is very apparent.
The high-mounted taillights were partly responsible for the car's
unusual appearance, but were very effective as a signaling device.
Don Bruno photo.

A European-registered V-6 sedan being used to tour the U.S. visits
a dealer for servicing. Author photo.

The European version of the Alfetta sedan was carbureted and had these large rectangular headlights and smaller, lighter bumpers. Mike Hemsley photo.

While the U.S. is only sent the six-cylinder version of the coupe, the four-cylinder model is still available in Europe as the GTV, with tail-lights, bumpers and trim upgraded to GTV6 components. Mike Hemsley photo.

Apparently even European owners like to "improve" their Alfas—here is a tarted-up four-door sedan. Mike Hemsley photo.

Alfa's Type 33 for the eighties was produced in an attempt to update and requalify the Alfasud as a high-quality, plush medium-size sedan. Sales have never reached expectations in Europe and the *Alfisti* say it doesn't excite like a 'Sud does. Alfa Romeo photo.

THE RARE AND DESIRABLE

A very real and genuine attraction that a performance-oriented company such as Alfa Romeo holds for the enthusiast is the manner in which special, limited production vehicles are proliferated and made available to individual owners. Many consider them to be the "true" Alfa Romeos—the vehicles the factory would prefer to be building if there were no external constraints. The emission standards and crash-test requirements enacted in the late sixties effectively ended the viability of routinely producing such special vehicles, at least at reasonable prices.

    The *very* rare Alfas of this chapter are hardly ever seen, seldom offered for sale and the most rewarding to own. They represent a distilled essence of the Alfa legend, a driveable chunk of history. It is frequently impossible to establish a price for such cars, particularly the one-offs. Some owners even refuse to enter negotiations for fear the temptation may prove to be too great.

The BAT Cars

Only three Berlina Aerodynamica Technica, or BAT, cars are known to have been constructed by Bertone and are intriguingly numbered BAT 5, BAT 7 and BAT 9. The BAT acronym was so appropriate that it couldn't possibly have been accidental, especially coming from the same people who gave us "Romeo and Giulietta." They are mechanically based on the 1900-Series cars, so parts will be somewhat available. Without question, they are **the** 1900 to have. Shown in various stages of restoration, from top to bottom, are BAT 5, 7 and 9, all of which are privately owned in the U.S. Bob Schnittger photos.

The 2000 Sportiva ★★★★★

Only four of the 2000 Sportivas were built in 1954 and 1955; two were coupes and two were roadsters. They were intended as competition vehicles but could easily have become a regular production car. The engine was based on the 1900, and the rear suspension featured a De-Dion axle with large inboard drum brakes. The Sportivas were quite aggressively styled, with a mix of Giulietta and Disco Volante lines. A production version would have been far more desirable than the 102-Series 2000 cars that finally did appear. At least one Sportiva is rumored to be in private hands, the rest at the factory museum. Tom Zat photo.

Factory Service Vans ★★★

ARI equipped a small fleet of Alfa Romeo vans to serve as mobile troubleshooting and training units in the U.S. The van itself is technically quite interesting. It has front-wheel drive, powered by a rear-facing Giulietta engine, with a driveshaft connecting it to a ZF four-speed transaxle. Without a rear drive axle, the van floor was built quite low to allow walk-in access from the back.

These service vans were barely able to maintain highway speed, and some were converted to 1600 engines by ARI. They were sold to individuals in the late sixties, and at least two of them are still together and running. Tom Tann photo.

6C-3000 CM ★★★★★

Six special vehicles—four coupes and two Spiders—were constructed in 1952 and 1953 using a new six-cylinder engine developed for a large sedan that never reached production. The C indicated competition usage, and the M designation reflected the engine modification from 2995 to 3495 cc displacement despite retaining the "3000" name. Horsepower was 246, and the factory used these cars for long-distance racing.

The coupe shown here was built to special order for Juan Peron with coachwork by Boano, and is now actively vintage raced in the U.S. by its owner, Henry Wessels III. The 6C-3000 Zagato Spider is the former Jo Bonnier car and is now in Japan. Henry Wessels III photos.

The Canguro ★★★★★

The Canguro was designed by Bertone as a more civilized, road-going version of the competition-oriented GTZ. The body was fiberglass, and the windows were flush with the body to maintain a high level of aerodynamic cleanliness. The interior was a lot more luxurious, but the overall weight was still held down to that of the GTZ. Of all the postwar cars that Alfa has chosen not to produce, the Canguro, or kangaroo, is the one whose loss elicits the greatest anguish among Alfa enthusiasts. Collectors should take note that the Canguro was sold after its impact as a show car wore off, and is now rumored to be privately owned in Europe.

The Farina TZ ★★★★★

Somewhat of a misnomer, the Farina TZ was another styling exercise on the GTZ tube-frame chassis. Designed by Pininfarina to be a street-able car in the same sense as the Canguro, the Farina TZ is also nicely finished and well-appointed. While the Canguro borrowed heavily from the styling of the GTZ, the Farina TZ took a very fresh approach, and looks like a blend of Sprint Speciale and 246 Dino. Like the Canguro, the Farina TZ was sold to an individual. It last came up for sale in California in 1982 with only a few thousand miles on the odometer, and was purchased by a very fortunate collector in Japan. Mike Ryan photo.

The 33 Stradale ★★★★★

Perhaps just to prove the versatility and relevance of its Type 33 Manufacturers' Prototype race cars, Alfa Romeo produced a road-going version. Known simply as the 33 Stradale, or street version, they are the most sensational of all the postwar streetable Alfas a collector could hope to own. Eighteen of these absolutely gorgeous coupes were built between 1967 and 1969 for "very special customers."

The body was fabricated in aluminum by Scaglione, and the engine was the two-liter, four-cam V-8 right out of the competition model. Only slightly detuned, it still produced 263 SAE horsepower. Weighing only 1,540 pounds, the 33 Stradale offers absolutely fierce performance. The racing transaxle is also used, making the 33 Stradale Alfa's only road car with six forward speeds.

The chassis of the Stradale was also used as the basis for five other Type 33-based show cars in the early seventies, but these vehicles have been retained by the factory for its museum. There are at least two privately owned 33 Stradales in the U.S. at this writing. Author photos.

The GT Am

When Group 2 production requirements of 1,000 vehicles effectively eliminated the GTA from competition in 1970, Alfa's response was to prepare a lightened, competition version of its production GTV coupe at Autodelta. The resulting car was designated the GT Am. The steel chassis and body of the 1750 GTV was used, with fiberglass hood, rear deck lid and doors. There was not even a pretext of providing an interior—these were to be stripped-shell race cars. Weight was reduced to about 2,000 pounds.

They were made with both 1750 and 2000 engines. The head was a twin-plug design similar to the GTA. Both Spica mechanical and Lucas slide-throttle injection systems were offered, and ratings of 220 SAE horsepower for the 1750 engine and 240 SAE for the 2000 engine were quoted. Special vented rotors and low-profile calipers were used to provide clearance for very wide 13-inch-diameter alloy wheels. In all, 40 GT Am's were built from 1970 to 1971. Too hot to be street driven, they could either be detuned or used primarily for track and show purposes. Author photos.

Type 33 Championship Cars ★★★★★

The Type 33 designation was applied to a long series of Alfa's Manufacturer Championship race cars, from the first two-liter V-8 version in 1967 through the three-liter, boxer twelve-cylinder cars of 1975 with which it won the series Championship. In other words, the Type 33 was used as a generic description for the Makes Championship cars, with suitable suffixes to describe the particular variation. Thus, the 33/2, 33/3 and 33 TT12 referred to the original two-liter, the three-liter of the 1969 to 1972 period and the final twelve-cylinder versions.

Many Type 33's have found their way into private hands and are being used for vintage racing and show purposes. Some are in museums; others are simply being held as an investment. The Type 33's are the last of the Sport-racing machinery Alfa turned out before re-entering Formula One competition. They inspired several road-going derivatives—the Montreal and 33 Stradale —and are the fastest and most exotic postwar Alfas one could ever hope to own. Tom Tann photos.

The Unofficial Alfas

When is an Alfa not an Alfa? Perhaps when there are no factory records acknowledging its existence. Private customers frequently commissioned coachbuilders to fabricate something special for them on an existing chassis. Motivations ranged from the desire to have a truly unique car, to an innovative solution to accident damage. To the collector these unofficial Alfas are highly desirable. They quite often possess a unique and often exciting history, and are regarded as rare and valuable treasures by their fortunate owners. Their hazy origins are no handicap, but reflect an earlier era when such practice was quite common.

Martin Zwig's beautiful 1900 Zagato shown here is such a car. Today it is actively vintage raced and was featured in the October '82 **Road & Track** coverage of the Mille Miglia. The 1900 Zagatos were primarily an arrangement between Zagato and private customers. Mike Roberts photo.

While the Giulietta Sprint Zagato was a factory-authorized series, its immediate predecessor was not. Ten vehicles known as the Giulietta SVZ were built by Zagato using existing Giulietta Sprint Veloces. The 1957 Series 1 coupe shown below is now in India. Photo from the Giulietta SZ register.

The Zagato-Bodied Alfas ★★★★★

The Zagato Alfas are worth considering again as a group, for they are a unique and wonderful phenomenon. Ever since the thirties, Zagato has produced special bodies for Alfa Romeo. The Zagato-Alfa collaboration has been particularly symbiotic and productive. The resulting cars are usually the most sporting model of a particular series, are limited in number, are technically very interesting, hand crafted and invariably become highly prized and excellent investments. A remarkable number of these vehicles are still in existence and many are within reasonable reach of the serious collector. Exciting and rewarding to own, the Zagato Alfas are true works of art and form a significant part of the Alfa legend. Author photo.

★★★★★

The 6C-2500 Competition Coupe
Three large, brutal-looking coupes were made from 1946 to 1950 based on the 6C-2500 chassis. At only 1,870 pounds, they were quite lightweight for their size. In racing trim, the six-cylinder engine produced 145 hp at 5500 rpm. Fangio drove one of these cars to third overall in the 1950 Mille Miglia, demonstrating its potential. In 1950, one of these coupes was modified to accept a new 6C-3000 engine based on the 1900 design, giving a twenty-two-horsepower gain. Any one of these Competition Coupes would be a delight to find, and would easily qualify as the most desirable 6C-2500. Factory photo courtesy of Bob Tucker.

What is it? Tom Zat of Alfa Heaven calls it an SSZ and plans a limited series of ten. Based on the Sprint Speciale, the body is modified, weight is reduced to 1,900 pounds, horsepower is almost 200, and the chassis is competition tuned. Still streetable, it has already been accepted for vintage racing by several Midwest organizations. Author photo.

PRICING GUIDE

These estimates of Alfa selling prices are simply an aid to help the interested buyer develop a feel for the approximate market value of these cars. They represent my own opinions and observations more than anything else, and should not be taken as a well-researched scientific effort. The low prices would apply to a running, usable vehicle, not a parts-car, while the high values are for the better-than-new, perfectly preserved models.

Although there are many published automotive pricing guides, the values they typically list for Alfas seem to be generally on the low side. The inclusion of dealer auction prices may partially account for this, along with a high percentage of personal transactions that are difficult to accurately document. I don't wish to argue with their statistics, but would love to find a few good Alfas at the bargain rates they sometimes suggest.

A couple of problems arise from this situation—it becomes harder to obtain bank financing on a good-condition Alfa, and it can be difficult to sell an Alfa to inexperienced buyers who base their offers solely on "book" value. Many of these price guides can be found in local book stores, and their information is updated on a regular basis. A few examples:

Old Car Value Guide Annual
by Quentin Craft Publications, Inc.

The Gold Book Quarterly
by Quentin Craft Publications, Inc.

Complete Book of Collectible Cars 1940-1980

The Red Book

The Blue Book

In addition, the authoritative reference used by insurance and banking professionals, *Cars of Particular Interest*, is an excellent but highly guarded resource. If your banker, broker or insurance agent won't help, try the library.

SUGGESTED PRICING (1986)

MODEL	LOW	AVERAGE	HIGH	MODEL	LOW	AVERAGE	HIGH
6C2500	$4,000	$ 8,000	$ 16,000	1750			
1900	1,500	7,000	14,000	Berlina	1,200	3,000	5,000
2000 (102)	500	3,500	7,000	GTV	1,200	3,500	7,500
2600 (106)				Spider Veloce	2,000	4,500	8,000
Berlina	1,200	4,500	8,000	2000 (105/115)			
Sprint	1,200	6,000	12,000	Berlina	1,200	3,000	5,000
Spider	1,200	6,000	12,000	GTV	2,000	4,000	10,000
Zagato	8,000	15,000	28,000	Spider Veloce	2,200	7,500	14,000
Giulietta				Alfetta			
Berlina	1,500	3,500	10,000	Sedan	1,500	2,400	3,000
Sprint	1,500	4,000	7,000	Sport Sedan	2,500	4,500	9,000
Sprint Veloce	1,500	5,000	10,000	GT, GTV	2,500	4,500	6,500
Spider	1,800	3,500	10,000	Sprint Veloce	3,500	6,500	9,000
Spider Veloce	2,000	5,000	15,000	GTV6	6,000	9,500	12,000
Sprint Speciale	4,500	8,000	18,000	Special			
Sprint Zagato	15,000	20,000	38,000	Montreal	10,000	13,000	18,000
Giulia				33 Stradale	90,000	140,000	200,000+
Sprint	1,500	2,400	6,000	Service Van	2,500	4,000	6,500
Spider	1,500	3,500	8,000	Milano	(new car pricing applies for 1986)		
Spider Veloce	1,500	5,500	10,000				
TI, Super	1,500	2,000	4,500				
Sprint GT, GTV	1,500	4,500	7,500				
Duetto	2,000	5,500	10,000				
Sprint Speciale	6,500	11,000	20,000				
GTZ	30,000	45,000	80,000				
Sprint GTA	12,000	18,000	25,000				
Sprint GTC	3,000	5,500	12,000				
Replicar	12,000	16,000	25,000				
TI Super	8,000	12,000	20,000				
GTA Junior	12,000	18,000	25,000				
Junior Z	5,000	8,000	15,000				
TZ 2	80,000	100,000	130,000				

CLUBS AND REGISTRIES

In addition to the two major North American Alfa clubs listed in the beginning of the book these following Alfa clubs are also available:

Alfa Romeo Association
San Francisco
28617 Miranda
Hayward, CA 94544

Dutch Alfa Romeo Owners Club
Ben Hendriks
Ruynemanstratt 56
5012 JH Tilburg
Holland

Alfa Romeo Owners Club of
  Australia
P.O. Box 216
Camberwell 3124
Victoria, Australia

Alfa Romeo Owners Club of New
  Zealand
33 Gray Ave.
Paraparaumu Beach
New Zealand

Cape Alfa Romeo Club
P.O. Box 804
Bellville 7530
Cape Town, Rep. of S. Africa

Alfa Club of Edmonton
P.O. Box 1484
Edmonton, Alberta T5J 2N7
Canada

AROC of Canada
John Winter
P.O. Box 62
Station Q
Toronto, M4T2L7
Canada

Puget Sound AROC
Terry Gates
8719 Green Avenue N.
Seattle, WA 98103

Alfa Romeo Owners Club of
  England
c/o Jill Maxted
Friars Way Cottage
Sheephatch Lane
Tilford, Farnham, Surrey,
England

Alfa Romeo Club de France
Bastarous
Chemin des Crete
64290 GAN
France

Swiss Alfa Romeo Register
Registre Suisse Alfa Romeo
Case Postale 196,
1000 Lausanne 12
Switzerland

As mentioned throughout the text, many of the rare or special interest Alfas have prompted the establishment of special registries or rosters. These groups serve to locate and document the condition of the cars, provide technical assistance, establish parts sources and help trace and authenticate the history of individual models. Membership in such a group is highly advisable if you own or are contemplating the purchase of a rare Alfa. While new registries are constantly being formed as the need arises, the ones presently in existence are:

Scuderia del Portello
c/o Alfa Romeo S.p.A.
Via Traiano, 35
20149 Milan
Italy
(factory vintage racing association, membership open to owners of qualifying vehicles)

6C2500/8C2900 Register
Malcolm Harris
999 Third Avenue
Suite 3210
Seattle, WA 98104

The 1900 Register
Peter Marshall
Mariners
Courtlands Avenue
Esher, Surrey KT10 9HZ
England

The Giulietta Register
Russ Baer
1729 Linden Avenue
Baltimore, MD 21217

The Giulietta Register
Tony Stevens
Ferncliffe, Openwoodgate
BELPER, Derbyshire DE5 1SB
England
(Includes 101 Giulias)

The Giulietta SZ Register
Donald E. Hughes/UMC
810 Twelfth Avenue S.
Nashville, TN 37203

The 200/2600 Register
Tom Zat
111 Zagato Lane
Aniwa, WI 54408

1300 & 1600 Spider Register
Chris Boles
406 King Court
Santa Paula, California 93060

Sprint Speciale Register
Leslie J. Hegedus
77 Christena Crescent
Pickering, ONT L1V 2K5
Canada

The Giulia T.I. Super Register
Donald A. Bruno
501 Irving Avenue
Hillside, Illinois 60162
(open to owners of any Giulia sedan)

GTA Register
Anders Ericsson
Vikingagatan 49
S-753 34 Uppsala
Sweden

Junior Zagato Register
Franco Macri
6 Oast House Road
Icklesham, Winchelsea
E. Sussex, England

Montreal Register
Gene Ross
P.O. Box 3925
Visalia, California 93287

The Montreal Register
Robert Winwood
Charni 20 E. Street
Quarry Bank, West Midlands
England

Zagato Car Club
Carrozzeria Zagato
20017 Terrazzano do Rho
Milano, Italy

The GTZ Register
George Pezold
73 Bay Avenue
Huntington, NY 11743

FACTORY SERVICE PUBLICATIONS

The following is a listing by ARI of the official service publications available for Alfa Romeos. They may usually be ordered through an authorized dealer.

Because of many similarities on the Alfa Romeo product line over the past years, some of the manuals are used for more than one model. Supplemental manuals define the differences among particular models.

OWNER'S MANUALS

The basic publication for instructions on the operation of your Alfa, the Owner's Manual also tells how to do minor tune-ups and contains a wiring diagram.

PUBL. #	TITLE	PRICE
772	Giulietta	$ 4.70
359	Giulia TI	4.70
978	Giulia Sprint GT (see #1170 below)	4.70
1065	Giulia Sprint GTA	40.00
1165	1600 Spider (105 series)	4.70
1170	Supplement to #978	4.70
1204	Giulia TI	4.70
1349	1300 Spider Jr.	4.70
1386	1750 Berlina, GTV, Spider, 1969	6.25
1490	1300 GT Jr.	4.70
1572	1750 Berlina, 1971	4.70
1639	1750 GTV, 1971	4.70
1640	1750 Spider, 1971	4.70
1845	2000 Berlina, 1972	4.70
1846	2000 GTV, 1972	4.70
1847	2000 Spider, 1972	4.70
2067	2000 Berlina, 1973	4.70
2068	2000 GTV, 1973	4.70
2069	2000 Spider, 1973	6.50
2191	2000 Berlina, 1974	4.70
2192	2000 GTV, 1974	4.70
2193	2000 Spider, 1974	4.70
2365	Alfetta 2000, 1975 '49 state'	4.70
2368	Alfetta GT 2000, 1975, '49 state'	4.70
2373	2000 Spider, 1975	4.70
2410	Alfetta 2000, 1976, 'Calif'	4.70
2411	Alfetta GT 2000, 1976, 'Calif'	4.70
2413	Alfetta 2000, 1976 '49 state'	4.70
2414	Alfetta GT 2000, 1976, '49 state'	7.50
2415	2000 Spider, 1976 '49 state'	4.70
2536	Sport Sedan, 1977 'Calif'	15.50
2540	2000 Spider, 1977 '49 state'	4.70
2541	Spider, 1977 'Calif'	12.00
2576	Sedan, 1978	4.70
2577	Sprint, 1978	4.70
2578	Spider, 1978	4.70
2679	Sedan, 1979	4.70
2680	Sprint, 1979	4.70
2681	Spider, 1979	4.70
2683	Sedan/Auto. 1979 - Supp. to 2679	4.70
2756	Spider, 1980	4.70
2857	Spider, 1981	
2870	GTV 6 2.5 1981	

PARTS CATALOGS

Complete reference of all component parts with illustrations and numbers. 1750 and 2000 series utilize USA supplements as master catalog is for European version.

PUBL. #	TITLE	PRICE
776/787	Giulietta models	$84.00
1251	1600 Spider (105 series)	22.75
1313	Giulia Sprint, GT, GTV, GTA, GTC	28.50
1380	1750 Berlina-European version	54.00
1387	1750 GTV, Spider-European version	41.50
1392	1750 Berlina-USA supplement	20.00
1393	1750 GTV, Spider-USA supplement	20.00
1517	1300 GT Jr.	20.25
1520	Giulia TI, TI Super, Super	36.50
1841	2000 Berlina-European version	38.50
1849	2000 GRV, Spider-European version	47.50
2006	2000 Berlina-USA supplement	14.25
2007	2000 GTV, Spider-USA supplement (72-74)	14.25
2007S	Supplement to #2007-USA Spider (75-77)	7.00
2266	Supplement to #2006-Factory Air Berlina	4.70
2454	Factory Air/Alfetta	4.70
2462	Alfetta USA version	8.00

WALL CHARTS

PUBL. #	TITLE	PRICE
1902	Wheel Alignment 105, 115 series	$ 7.25
1944	Transaxle-Alfetta models	7.25
2016	Rear Suspension-Alfetta models	7.25
2169	Front Suspension-Alfetta models	7.25
2429	Cutaway drive train-Alfetta models	7.25

TECHNICAL INSPECTION SPECIFICATIONS

Contains dimensions, specifications and information for each model vehicle for inspecting components.

All prices are suggested retail and subject to change without notice.

PUBL. #	TITLE	PRICE
955	Giulia 1600 'normale' versions	4.10
1133	Giulia Super	4.10
1210	Giulia Sprint GTV	4.10
1212	1600 Spider (105 series)	4.10
1226	1300 GT Jr.	4.10
1366	1300 Spider Jr.	4.10
1370	1300 GTA Jr.	4.10
1502	1750 USA models, 1969	4.10
2106	2000 models, 1972-4	4.10
2364	Alfetta 2000, 1975-76 '49 state'	6.75
2438	Alfetta 2000, 1976 'Calif' versions (supplement to #2364 above)	4.10
2663	Automatic Alfetta Sedan	9.50
2760	Sedan Coupe 1975-8	5.00
2910	GTV 6 2.5 1981	

SUGGESTED READING

Alfissimo! by David Owen
A pleasant reading book that explores the design, manufacturing and political philosophies shaping the cars of Alfa Romeo. While concentrating on postwar vehicles, Alfa's early history is briefly covered as background for understanding the company's present directions.

Alfa Romeo—All Cars From 1910 by Luigi Fusi
A model-by-model description of every Alfa built up to 1977. This is *the* authoritative text on Alfas by a man who helped build them. Besides many years of running Alfa's prototype shop, Mr. Fusi was charged with the establishment of the factory historical museum. This is a reference that no serious Alfa collector should be without.

Alfa Romeo by Peter Hull
An interesting historical treatment of Alfa's early history, with primary emphasis on its competition achievements.

Famous Automobile Museums No. 1: Museo Alfa Romeo
A photographic collection of the cars displayed in Alfa Romeo's historical museum, plus some tantalizing views of the beautiful museum building itself. Text in Japanese and English.

AFTERMARKET PARTS AND SERVICES

AFRA
Via Carraciola #24
Milano, Italy 20155
Outlet for obsolete factory parts—excellent source for hard-to-find older items. If all else fails, try AFRA. Staff will correspond in English or Italian; specify model and part numbers in your inquiry.

Alfacenta
Turgis Green
Basingstoke
Hants
RG27 OAG
Tel. 0256 882831
Spares for 1960-1980 Alfas

Alfa Heaven
111 Zagato Ln
Aniwa, WI 54408
(715) 449-2141
Tom Zat's Alfa restoration service, plus new and used parts for older Alfas. Specializes in Giulietta and 2600 models, publishes the 200/2600 newsletter, operates an AROC tech hotline for member problems.

Alfa Performance Connection
3800 Campus Dr, St. D
Newport Beach, CA
(714) 852-0822
Independent Alfa servicing by Stewart Sandeman, Tech Advisor for *Alfa Owner*, operates an AROC tech hotline for member problems.

Alfa Ricambi
6640 San Fernando Rd
Glendale, CA 91201
(213) 246-7263
Mail-order Alfa parts, specialist in old 2000 and 2600 components

Alfetta Racing Centre Ltd.
Swan Works
416-418 London Road
Isleworth
Middlesex
Tel. 01-560 6194
Repairs, Restoration & Spares For Italian High Performance Cars

Autovolante
4410 SW 74th Ave
Miami, FL 33155
(305) 261-8481
Mail-order Alfa parts, specialist in fiberglass body panels

Barber's Shop
1116 18th St
Sacramento, CA 95814
(916) 448-6422
Specialty shop for servicing and performance work on Alfas

Benalfa Cars
5 Washington Road
West Wilts Trading Estate
Westbury
Wilts
Tel. 0373 864333
Tuning—Servicing—Major Overhauls (inc. Bodywork)

Black Bart's Auto Emporium
3917 Northrup
Ft. Wayne, IN 46805
(219) 484-5511
Mail-order Alfa parts, specialist in older Alfas, particularly 1900's, good source for hard-to-find carburetor and hydraulic rebuild kits and components

Bobcor Imports
241 N. Washington Ave
Bergenfield, NJ 07621
(201) 387-7777
A dealer specializing in mail-order original equipment parts, performance components and "boutique" items. Sponsors Bobcor Alfa Club, has excellent catalog.

Centerline Products, Inc
Box 1466
Boulder, CO 80306
(303) 447-0239
Mail-order Alfa parts, rebuild service for Spica fuel pumps

Classic Motorbooks, Inc
P.O. Box 1
Osceola, WI 54020
(715) 294-3345
Workshop manuals and literature

E. B. Spares
2 Washington Road
West Wilts Trading Estate
Westbury Wilts
Tel. 0373 823856
Alfa Romeo Spares

Ereminas Imports, Inc
Clearview Ave
Harwinton, CT 06791
(203) 485-9800
Mail-order Alfa parts going back through Giulietta, specialist in hard-to-find items. Manufactures reproductions of unavailable original equipment such as Veloce headers, rubber gaskets and rocker panels.

FAZA
149 Powell Ave
Southampton, NY 11968
(516) 283-1283
Daytona exhaust systems to fit many older Alfa models, alloy wheels

International Autoparts
1309 Mountain View St
Charlottesville, VA 22901
(804) 295-0127
Mail-order Alfa parts going back through Giulietta, good selection of rebuilt electrical components

JAFCO Turbocharging Systems
Dept AO
3016 B Halladay St
Santa Ana, CA 92705
(714) 641-5881
Specialist in turbocharger system kits for injected Alfas, several stages available

PAECO Industries
213 South 21st St
Birmingham, AL 35233
(205) 323-8376
Rebuilt Alfa engines in any state of tune up to full competition

Serra
P.O. Box 296
279 Adams St
Bedford Hills, NY 10507
Weber kits, performance cams and pistons, rebuilds and restorations for Alfas

Shankle Automotive Engineering
9135-F Alabama Ave
Chatsworth, CA 91311
Mail-order Alfa parts, designs and manufactures many specialty items to mechanically enhance Alfas, Weber conversions, 203 HP turbo kit, excellent catalog

Stephen Victor Ltd.
Specialist Motor Engineers
off Old Town
Clapham
London SW4
Tel. 01-720 6131
Franchised Alfa Romeo Service And Parts Dealer

Valco Enterprises, Inc
13566 Floyd Circle, Suite E
Dallas, TX 75243
(214) 234-5144
Specialty shop for servicing and performance work on Alfas, good stock of used parts, mail-order service parts

Ward and Deane Racing
115 N. Oak St. #15
Inglewood, CA 90301
(213) 649-5369
High performance suspension systems for Alfas, plus racing and heavy-duty components